Publisher's Note

In many ways, the cover of this book belongs to Frank MacConnell. At a "town hall" meeting in June 1995, MacConnell asked Speaker of the House Newt Gingrich and President Bill Clinton if they would pursue the formation of a blue-ribbon panel—much like the one that decided on military base closings—to create a plan to reform the nation's campaign finance system. Congress would then vote yes or no on the plan and not be permitted to amend it. Clinton and Gingrich shook hands on the deal and committed to the appointment of such a commission.

They lied.

The clearest indication that they lied is that no such commission was ever formed. The president sent the speaker a letter outlining his proposed structure of the commission. The speaker rejected it as a political gimmick and maintained other priorities were claiming his time. Both men began playing the "blame game." Does anyone truly believe that the most powerful person in the legislative branch and the most powerful person in the executive branch could not have formed the blue-ribbon group if they really had meant to do so?

Frank MacConnell, so full of hope on that day, saw the lie flourish, and he died in 1996 without seeing his wish fulfilled. Campaign finance reform continues to be killed at every opportunity by Washington politicians and by the men who shook hands on that sunny day in Claremont, New Hampshire. They themselves are tainted by the very system they purport to want to reform. They are men who lie and who fail to lead the nation out of a system that continues to rob America of its hope for a better democracy.

The hope Cecil Heftel, a five-term member of Congress from Hawaii, promotes in this book is to end the corruption, what he calls "legalized bribery." Heftel outlines a simple, effective alternative to the dominance of special interests. It's a proposal that will help put power back where it belongs: in the hands of the American people.

Praise for

End Legalized Bribery

"It is a timely book, and one that I hope will help to encourage and focus efforts to clean up the disgrace of uncontrolled campaign financing. Coming from someone who knows the facts, it's especially valuable."

—JIMMY CARTER
Former President of the United States

"Cecil Heftel puts his expertise to work on the issue Americans must solve if we are to save our democratic system of government, campaign finance reform. He's tired of hearing nothing can be done and lays out a plan. GO CECIL!"

—PAT SCHROEDER
President and CEO, Association of American Publishers
Former member, U.S. House of Representatives

"If you want to get on top of how the corruption of money in politics affects your country and your living standards, former Congressman Cecil Heftel's book, *End Legalized Bribery*, is just the concise, vivid, and very memorable volume you need. Most ex-Representatives choose not to remember after they leave office. Mr. Heftel remembers because he wants to get rid of money (mostly from business interests) that nullifies or makes your votes meaningless. Then he shows how you can be part of this Great Reform."

—RALPH NADER
Consumer Advocate

"An honest and totally candid recounting of where our system of campaign finance has led us."

—JOHN ANDERSON
Professor of Law, Nova Southeastern University Law Center
Former member, U.S. House of Representatives and
Presidential Candidate

"A candid, straightforward analysis of a major national problem."

—PAUL SIMON
Director of the Public Policy Institute, Southern Illinois University
Retired U.S. Senator, Illinois

"In the U.S. House of Representatives where he and I were colleagues for many years, Cecil Heftel took on the tough, timely issues without the usual Congressional formality and folderol. So it doesn't surprise me a bit that Cec, in his new book, *End Legalized Bribery*, takes on the toughest, timeliest issue of the day—money and politics nor that he does so in his patented 'pull no punches,' 'let's get down to brass tacks' style.

"Since nuanced, subtle analysis has not yielded much success in ridding politics of the corrosive, corrupting influence of unbridled, unregulated campaign money, maybe Cec's 'in your face' approach will do the job. I certainly hope so!

"In any event, we all owe Cec a debt of gratitude for taking the lead in purging the political system of the accumulated filth of campaign finance abuses."

—ROMANO MAZZOLI
Former Member, U.S. House of Representatives

"Cecil Heftel gives a first-hand account of how good people are trapped in a bad system. And he presents a plan for eliminating the legalized graft and corruption allowed under our current campaign finance system."

—RUSSELL J. VERNEY
Chairman, Reform Party of the United States of America

"At one time, the title of this book would have been a hyperbole. Today, tragically, it is reality. A great nation can get the correct answers out of a corruptible system."

—RICHARD LAMM
Former Governor of Colorado

"You have to commend Cecil Heftel on his honesty. He explains in plain language for everyone to understand what campaign reform is all about and how it can work. It was amazing as I read the book, I could almost hear Frank saying the same thing."

—JEAN MACCONNELL
Sullivan County Commissioner
Widow of Frank MacConnell, the New Hampshirite who asked the question that prompted the now infamous handshake and pledge by President Clinton and Speaker Gingrich to appoint a bipartisan panel on political finance and lobbying reforms

"Read this book and weep. The campaign system in America is screwed up. When enough people understand this, things will change."

—JERRY BROWN
Mayor-elect of Oakland, California
Former Governor of California

"Americans have a penchant for telling other people how to run free elections. But how accurately do U.S. elections represent the true feelings of the American people? Far fewer Americans vote than electors in most other democracies. And, shamefully, American votes more and more can be bought by candidates, especially incumbents, able to generate tens of millions of dollars to purchase television time.

"In Britain where I was elected to Parliament nine times over 27 years, it is illegal—and unthinkable!—that those who seek high office should be able to use money to gain unfair advantage over their opponents.

"Congressman Heftel has done a great service in exposing the travesty of democracy that money politics is bringing to America. It is high time that Americans saw their campaign finance malpractices as others see them."

—SIR ELDON GRIFFITHS
President, Orange County World Affairs Council
Former Member of the British House of Commons

"Cecil Heftel's inside view of our corruptive campaign finance practices is insightful and provocative; his Clean Money Campaign plan deserves a hearing."

—ROBERT P. SIGMAN
Editorial Board, *The Kansas City Star*

"Former Congressman Cecil Heftel's book documents how the present system of campaign finance has led to billions and billions in subsidies to large corporations at the expense of the average taxpayer. Was our national security compromised by campaign contributions in 1996? Present members of Congress have no interest in changing a system which they are the beneficiaries of.

"Only when people get aroused to action will we see an end to this scandalous system. *End Legalized Bribery* will inform people as to the abuses of our current system and a new 'Clean Campaign' finance system."

—THOMAS L. JUDGE
Former Governor of Montana

End Legalized Bribery

End Legalized Bribery

An Ex-Congressman's
Proposal to Clean Up Congress

CECIL HEFTEL

SEVEN LOCKS PRESS
SANTA ANA, CALIFORNIA
MINNEAPOLIS, MINNESOTA
WASHINGTON, D.C.

Library of Congress Cataloging-in-Publication Data
Heftel, Cecil. 1925–
     End legalized bribery: an ex-congressman's proposal to clean up
Congress / by Cecil Heftel.
        p. cm.
     ISBN 0-929765-59-1
     1. Campaign funds—Untied States. 2. Political corruption—
United States. I. Title.
JK1991.H43   1998
324.7'8'0973—dc21   98-17982
                                            CIP

Manufactured in the United States of America
Seven Locks Press
P.O. Box 25689
Santa Ana, California 92799
(800) 354-5348

Dedication

For Joyce and her many years of dedication and assistance and for my children Cathy, Lani, Peggy, Susan, Chris, Terry, and Richard. For Marty Jezer and Margaret Engle. For the personal dedication and professional contribution of my former congressional aides and directors Jessica Kirk, Laura Figueira, Carmen Cantorna, and Margaret Shean and loyal supporters C. R. Fuller and Gina Schultz. In appreciation of their support, hard work, and loyalty.

For the future
My grandchildren
And your grandchildren

In Memoriam

CARMEN CANTORNA

During the drafting of this book, Carmen Cantorna, my loyal and dedicated assistant, who dedicated her life to the service of Hawaii, passed away. Her very devoted daughter, Cindy, was with her night and day during the last months of her life. Carmen was dearly beloved by all of us who had the privilege of working with her, and she earned the eternal gratitude of all of the thousands of residents of Hawaii who came in contact with her.

Contents

Foreword

I serve on the national advisory board of the Public Policy Institute of Southern Illinois University. The director is former Senator Paul Simon from my home state of Illinois. Recently, the institute announced that two of the key items on its 1998 agenda were combating the portrayal of violence on television and reforming the way American political campaigns are funded. It occurred to me as I read the announcement that violence is the key common element of these two public policy issues. On television, the senseless, repetitious depiction of human depravity becomes so commonplace that it dulls our sense of moral outrage. In the political realm, vote-buying and influence peddling under the false and misleading label of political contributions do violence to the most basic concepts of our democratic form of representative government.

As 1997 drew to a close and these lines were being written, we confronted as a nation a great anomaly, reflected by an outpouring of statistics. The so-called misery index—the combined annual rates of inflation and unemployment—was the lowest in almost a quarter of a century. Even as the contagion of the so-called Asian flu roiled the currency markets and stock exchanges of nations on the other side of the world, the American economy appeared to be robust and the envy of every other country on the face of the globe. However, poll after poll showed that a distrustful public held its institutions of government, to use the phrase employed by a former speaker of the House of Representatives to show his disdain for an errant member, in "minimum high regard." Less elegantly phrased, the political air in our beloved country is redolent with the stench of corruption as revelations are made of how big money influenced the conduct of the most recent presidential and congressional elections. Yes, today most Americans believe that, in Shakespeare's prose, "there is something rotten in the state of Denmark." Yes, the economy may be sound, but in our heart of hearts we know that our electoral process is tragically flawed, and unless we awaken to the task of changing it, our democracy itself is in peril.

In the chapters of Cecil Heftel's book on the need for campaign finance reform, you see revealed his passionate commitment to the task of being a leader in that cause. A number of books over the past decade have addressed the problem, and, as does the author of this book, I pay tribute to those efforts to awaken the American people to the danger of continuing on our present course. However, what makes this book unique and so stirring a call for reform is the persona of the author and the qualifications he possesses to deal with the subject matter of campaigns and how they should be financed. He knows whereof he speaks.

A self-made multimillionaire, Cecil Heftel understands what motivates those from the business community who contributed in 1996 to the most costly elections in our history. As a dedicated public servant who five times was selected by the people of Hawaii to represent them in the Congress of the United States, he witnessed firsthand the corrupting influence of the money-chase in terms of the dependence it created in those who became literally trapped by the demands of increasingly higher-cost campaigns. He does not, however, simply rely on sweeping generalizations based merely on anecdotal evidence. Such sources as the Center for Responsive Politics provide solid documentation for the charges the author makes.

As a former member of the House Ways and Means Committee, my former congressional colleague Cecil Heftel was in a particularly strategic position to observe how our tax laws are made. His chapter 6, "Campaign Contributions and Unfair Taxes," is a devastating indictment of the inequities that exist in our tax system and the indisputable link with the system whereby private money has established an exaggerated influence on public policy. Succeeding chapters, which portray the same kind of link between campaign dollars and how the public's hard-earned dollars are allocated in areas such as defense policy, health care, and efforts to protect the environment, are just as revealing. You begin to understand the depth of Cecil Heftel's congealed rage that we are traducing the most basic and elemental principles of representative democracy in the way our elected representatives have become hirelings of a vast panoply of special interests.

Fortunately for the reader and for America as well, *End Legalized Bribery* does not end here. Cecil Heftel's book does not conclude with only a litany of despair. Rather, in specific terms he lays down a prescription for reform. He does not do so in some vague, exhortative call for change without providing the direction in which we must go to return to the high road that our Founding Fathers attempted to chart for us. In detailing the "Clean Money Option" where private money can be substituted by a program of public funding at a reasonable level (he estimates at a cost of $6.50 a year for each person of voting age in the United States) he offers genuine hope for real reform. Even though recent reform efforts have faltered, Cecil Heftel's *End Legalized Bribery* should inspire the American public to believe that there is a way out of the present morass.

I hope—and I know with absolute certainty that this is why this book was written—this honest and totally candid recounting of where our system of campaign finance has led us will energize concerned citizens across America to help our beloved country find a new way. I heard Elizabeth Arnold of National Public Radio say that the Congress seems to be waiting for a groundswell from the American people before it acts. Armed with the knowledge and the irrefutable arguments presented in *End Legalized Bribery*, the American people can now effectively launch that groundswell.

John Anderson
Former Member
U.S. House of Representatives

Crisis Prevention

I should have finished this book long before now. I would have had it done in 1994 if the Republicans had not won a majority in both houses of Congress that year and ended what was effectively forty years of Democratic control of the national legislature. Upon that electoral victory by the GOP, I stopped the writing process. I should have pressed on because nothing changed. My thesis had been that four decades of Democratic reign had yielded worse than nothing. In fact, the tenure of the Democratic party had engendered a tremendous distrust among the American people toward Congress and led the entire Congress to foster an economic debacle from which the nation is still recovering, even as the mismanagement continues. As our long rebound shows, I severely underestimated—and am thankful that I did—the capacity of our economy to withstand the ineptitude of our national government. Still, imagine how much better off we all would be if Congress had been intent on serving the nation's interest, on putting the people first.

During my ten years in Congress, I learned that the reason for the ineffectiveness and the damage Congress kept causing the nation was directly tied to the responsiveness of its members—particularly the leadership in both parties—not to the national interest, but to the special interests that contributed to politicians' election campaigns. Instead of taking advantage of an opportunity to show that things could be done differently, that politics could be improved, the new Republican majority immediately began to demonstrate that it had learned well from the Democrats. Instead of denouncing the system that had rendered Congress *un*representative of the national interest, the new majority simply adopted the behavior of the former majority. This tragic system continues today, and there has been no credible evidence to indicate that it will change anytime soon.

Members of Congress—caught in a system requiring that the first thing they do when they arrive on Capitol Hill is learn how to raise money for reelection—court, cajole, pressure, and even extort special interests in return for access, influence, and action on matters of direct concern to those interests. While many individual members have exhibited great integrity within this cesspool of influence peddling, few escape it entirely. The rules of the game are clear: Raise enough money as an incumbent and you'll likely have a long, prosperous career on the Hill and beyond. Little wonder that the leadership, usually members who have long tenure, chooses to "lead" in a direction other than reform of a system that is severely broken.

These rules are clear not only to members of Congress but also to their patrons, the special interests that contribute to their campaigns and expect something in return. Whether it is a business, a labor union, a so-called public interest group, a religious organization, or a civic organization, any group willing to give some money usually does so in an effort to gain an advantage in the debate on issues of importance great and small to the nation. The patrons are not always corporations—although in pure dollar amounts the business sector gives the most—and they should not be especially vilified nor will I attempt to do that. I have had far too much success in business to believe that business is evil. Quite the contrary. Businesses have begun to realize that the whole process is something of a shakedown, but they also understand that they must get things done efficiently and effectively, and if investing money helps to cut through the red tape and make sure their point of view is heard, the temptation is great.

The relatively small contribution is often worth what I call the "return on investment."

Now, whether it is business or labor or a civic group doing the giving, if the giving is done for the purpose of gaining *special* advantage in the debate, then the money is being used to distort the debate. That is plain wrong, but it is the way the system is designed to function. Quite often, similar groups on different sides of a single issue pour money into the debate. It is just Washington "business as usual," and a campaign contribution—considered to be a bribe in other parts of our society—is just another cost of doing business, even if it's not a business doing the giving. The problem, of course, is that such participation perpetuates a corrupt, antidemocratic way of conducting the *nation's* business.

I learned two immensely important lessons during my years in Washington. First, Congress responds directly to public opinion. Second, Congress rarely acts until there is a push-come-to-shove kind of crisis. Too often, as I saw first-hand with the savings and loan mess, Congress actually creates the crisis.

These days, during relatively prosperous economic times for most of the country, there might seem to be little concern about deficits and government waste. This is when Congress can be at its most dangerous, when it gets a relatively free ride. Intellectually, people recognize that the campaign finance system ultimately costs them money, that if Congress would not so easily accommodate the special interests, then all our taxes might be lower and the national deficit smaller. But the fervor to do something about it and a consensus on what to do have yet to emerge because most of us are pretty comfortable. The nation is not in an economic crisis or in a constitutional crisis the likes of Watergate. So mobilizing public opinion to reform the way campaigns are financed will be a challenge. My question is, Why do we want to wait for a crisis before we start fixing the very problem that will help create one?

CHAPTER ONE

Big Money, Bad Politics

(or, It's Just Legal Bribery)

Of all the mischiefs, none is so afflicting and fatal to every honest hope as the corruption of the legislature.

— THOMAS JEFFERSON

It is Money! Money! Money! Not ideas, not principles, but money that reigns supreme in American politics!

— SENATOR ROBERT C. BYRD (D-WV)

In the wake of the 1996 election, the scandal of money in politics suddenly became newspaper headlines. Republicans claimed that the Democrats raised money illegally. Democrats claimed that the Republicans did the same. Congressional hearings were held. There was much partisan bickering and outrage. The president was accused of offering a night in a White House bedroom in exchange for large donations to the Democratic Party. Apparently, in the Clinton White House, large contributors to the Democratic Party, no matter how sleazy their reputation, could arrange for a private presidential meeting.

In what have become the perverse ways of conducting public discourse in Washington, the Republican congressional leadership made the current administration's problems with campaign finances an opportunity to get revenge for Watergate. Vice President Al Gore was accused of making fund-raising phone calls from the White House, an improper and stupid act, the stupidity of which Gore only compounded by stating there was "no controlling legal authority" for the phone calls made from a government office. One of the first things freshman members of Congress learn is that making fund-raising calls from their offices is illegal. Gore was essentially claiming that such laws do not apply to the White House. This matter, along with the allegation that Gore tried to raise campaign funds from Buddhist nuns and the counterclaims by Democrats of unethical behavior on the part of Republicans, has reduced politics to a constant blame game.

What President Clinton and Vice President Gore or what Republican leaders did to raise money in 1996 may or may not have been illegal. The courts will decide that, and public opinion will weigh in on the matter as well. Yet the big problem of our money-driven politics is not so much that which is *illegal*, it's that which is *legal*. Hundreds of millions of dollars are given to political candidates by a small wealthy elite (less than 1 percent of the population) in order to promote their own vested economic interests in public affairs—that's the problem.

It's hypocritical to squander millions of dollars in congressional investigations to embarrass members of the opposing party and then reject any effort to reform the system of campaign finance reform that is responsible for the scandals. Indeed, despite the headlines about corruption in the campaign system and the feigned outrage of partisan politicians, they and their parties continue unashamedly to raise campaign contributions as if there were no scandal, as if the public didn't care. And groups and individuals with vested interests in government continue to ply candidates with money as if selling and buying influence in government were standard political procedure, the way politics gets done. The tragedy is that all of this is standard, just the way business is done.

The congressional investigations were a sham meant to gain headlines at the expense of meaningful reform—and the public knows this. In a poll conducted by *The Los Angeles Times* in September 1997, when the Senate investigation was at its height, almost three-quarters of the respondents (73 percent) said that both political parties were guilty of campaign finance abuses during the 1996 election. More than 60 percent called for some form of campaign finance reform.

The campaign system is a travesty of democracy. I say this not as an angry outsider envious of other people's power. From 1977 through 1986, I represented the First District of Hawaii in the United States House of Representatives. I know how to play the game of politics and how to play it well. Moreover, as a successful businessman, I had the personal financial resources to run and win races for political office; I am not naive about the importance of money in politics. Had I not been able to spend my own money, I would never have had the resources to win elective office. The simple fact is this: money not only fuels campaigns, it often decides them. Big money largely designates who runs, who wins, what issues are raised, how they are framed, and finally, how legislation is drafted.

Without money and lots of it, success is next to impossible in American politics. A candidate either has to be independently wealthy, as I was, or have the ability to raise money from people who have wealth. And the latter ultimately means doing the bidding of those who give large campaign contributions. Big donors are essential to electoral success. That is why so many politicians—even the honest ones who want to do good for the people—often wind up in the pockets of fat-cat funders.

In order to run for high-level elective office today, candidates have to begin preparations years before the actual race. If they do not have their own money, the first thing they have to do is go out and raise it. Prospective candidates must court total strangers and convince

3

them, by telephone or in person, that with money, their candidacy will be viable and credible. Candidates must also make it clear that they will advance the positions their new benefactors are known to support. Many politicians are good at this and take great satisfaction in their ability to talk strangers into giving them money to run for office. Others find the experience humiliating. They do not like the idea of selling themselves. They do not believe an ability to raise money should be a necessary qualification for holding public office.

The necessity of raising money to run for office is a kind of election in itself. Instead of submitting themselves to voters who need only pull a lever or fill in a ballot to register an opinion, prospective candidates have to submit themselves to wealthy people or to political action committees (PACs) who register their support with cash contributions. These fat cats and PACs exist as an unofficial screening committee of American elections. Candidates who do not garner fat-cat and PAC approval usually do not have the money to wage competitive campaigns and, therefore, do not win public office.

This limits voters' choices. The only candidates they can vote for are the ones who have been preapproved by the rich and powerful. Is it any wonder that less than 50 percent of all eligible voters bother to cast a ballot? Some pundits blame apathy. I would suggest that the refusal to vote, while regrettable, is a conscious decision. Why should voters want to choose between candidates who have been preselected for them and who, in order to have enough money to run credible campaigns, must win the approval of groups and individuals that have their own interests at heart, not those of the American people? There has to be a way for candidates to run for office without having to sell their souls to the big-money operators. There has to be a way for honest individuals to run for and hold office without sacrificing their principles.

In my experience, most members of Congress are honest and hard working. Most of them go to Washington with good intentions, but once there they enter a cesspool. Even the world's most righteous, scrupulous people would probably be compromised by the process of running for office. For it's hard to do the right thing in a system in which the raising of money is the prerequisite of success. And it's hard to work for the greater good in a system that practically forces candidates to do the bidding of the special interests that provide them with money. Indeed, the source of many of the worst failings of the American government is the campaign finance system as we know it.

Today's campaign finance laws promote begging, bribery, and extortion. The problem—in both congressional and presidential campaigns, as well as state and local elections—is that there are no limits to what a contributor can give and what a candidate can take in running for office. There are so-called limits, of course, contribution limits that are written as law. But the loopholes—as understood by those who created them—are so large and obvious that for all intents and purposes the limits do not exist. What's deemed illegal in every other aspect of life is considered legal in campaigns for political office. I find this outrageous and I'm sure you do too. That is why we need real campaign finance reform that puts an end to the corrupting influence of big money in American politics.

Imagine, if you will, a criminal defendant on trial approaching the jury just before sentencing and handing each member a bag full of money. There's no question such a move would be viewed as attempted bribery for which that criminal would be severely punished. When a contractor agrees to buy materials from a certain vendor in exchange for a little extra money slipped under the table, the transaction is viewed as an illegal kickback. When gamblers bribe athletes into throwing a game or shaving points, they are committing a crime and everybody knows it. If caught, the participants in all these slippery deals would likely end up in jail.

Every day in Washington, lobbyists or corporate executives who have a financial stake in public policy give elected officials thousands—even hundreds of thousands—of dollars and expect, in return, to be given special consideration when legislation affecting their businesses is up for consideration. Yet, since the money that changes hands is a campaign contribution, it is perfectly legal.

Let me explain this from a more personal perspective. In the 1950s, shortly after I got out of the Army (I am a veteran of World War II), I saw an opportunity to invest in radio stations. Television was gaining in popularity and many radio station owners, thinking they could not compete with this new broadcast medium, were willing to sell their radio stations cheap. This was also the period when rock 'n' roll was just becoming popular. As a result, the popularity of radio was revived. Adults, forgetting their own youth, are all too often shocked by the music favored by their children. In the 1950s there were many adults who did not approve of Elvis Presley's swiveling hips. We then lived in a totally segregated society in which racist attitudes were upheld by the force of law, and there were many white people in positions of authority who did not like the fact that millions of white teenagers were coming of age listening to what—at least before Elvis—was an exclusively black form of popular music. Consequently, there was an effort by some members of Congress to discourage radio stations from playing rock 'n' roll.

At the time it was common for record companies to give under-the-table gifts to disc jockeys in order to get them to play their records. "Payola" it was called, and strictly speaking it was a kind of bribery. In an attempt to attack rock music and harass the upstart radio stations playing it, Congress held hearings that criminalized the practice of payola. In the aftermath of this so-called payola scandal, quite a few disc jockeys and program managers lost their jobs in radio. A few even went to jail.

As a breach of ethics, taking payola for playing rock 'n' roll was petty stuff and harmless too. Little Richard and Elvis Presley would have been popular whether or not record companies bribed disc jockeys with a bottle of scotch and $50 to play their records. How important is record company payola compared to the millions of dollars special interests give and political candidates take in every campaign season? Why is it illegal to bribe a disc jockey but legal to bribe a candidate for public office? Which is worse: bribing a disc jockey or bribing a politician? What is more important: paying money to play a

6

record or paying money to influence public policy? In my opinion, campaign contributions are political payola. Bribery is immoral no matter whom it benefits.

Political payola is not given randomly. There is clearly a connection between campaign contributions from special interest groups and carefully crafted legislation. It is something I want to emphasize now and throughout this book: *Money pours into political campaigns from out-of-state interests and from contributors who have little in common with the voters in a candidate's state or district.* Interest groups funnel money to political incumbents who have jurisdiction over issues that affect them most. Banking and financial interests give most of their money to members of Congress who sit on committees dealing with financial and banking matters. Agribusiness interests give to members on agricultural committees. Defense contractors give to members dealing with military issues. Oil companies give to members dealing with natural resource and energy issues, and so forth. In return for that money, which pays for the glossy, high-profile campaigns that win votes, members of Congress promote and pass legislation that benefits their big donors instead of their constituents.

Many funders and politicians believe there is nothing wrong with candidates taking special interest money. "That is the way the system works," they will say when challenged. And indeed, they are right. Ever since the country began, individuals and organizations with financial interests in governmental affairs have been financing the ambitions of political candidates by giving money to the candidates and their parties. From the standpoint of those who do it, it is simply the way you get things done. It's the cost of doing business in Washington, as it is in state capitols and municipal city halls.

Candidates and interest groups would lead us to believe that access—the sort of access that is bought with a campaign contribution—is innocent. They might even say that when lobbyists representing interest groups meet with elected officials all they do is talk about sports, movies, their children, maybe the weather—a bunch of good old boys sitting around a congressional office chewing the fat. But members of Congress are too busy and lobbyists too determined for idle small talk.

Even if I had never served a day in Congress, I would know—as you know—that when special interests make substantial contributions to members of Congress or to any other elected official, they are buying an opportunity to influence public policy in return for that contribution. In other words, they are "buying access." Access—what a concise word for something with such messy consequences. What special interests want and contribute money to obtain is a chance to talk directly with elected officials about the public policies affecting their business. More importantly and more specifically, special interests want elected officials to write laws that support their particular business or industry and to disregard the effect those laws may have on individuals, the general public, or the country.

No matter what the issue—whether it be balancing the budget to keep our country economically viable, reforming the tax structure, investing in infrastructure and jobs so the country can function and our citizens will have work, building a strong military to keep our country safe, protecting family farms, preserving the integrity of our banking system, creating a pollution-free environment, making health care available to all—money talks more loudly than the voice of the American people.

How does this affect ordinary, cash-strapped citizens who grind through life paying taxes, voting in elections, and working hard to make ends meet?

- It means their needs are too often unmet and their voices are too often not heard, at least in Washington.

- It means that public officials elected to represent all the people are more attuned to the wants and words of the few who donated heavily during their campaigns.

- It means that legislation is skewed to favor the special interests, to give them what they, not the general public, need and want.

8

- It means that you pay, through higher taxes and the cost of prejudicial legislation, for the lucrative tax breaks and subsidies big contributors get as payback.

It means, in short, that special interests—and that includes special individuals—wind up making money and increasing their power while ordinary citizens wind up losing money, power, and confidence in their future.

The benefits big contributors get in return for the money they give come in the form of tax breaks and subsidies specifically engineered to give their businesses an easy economic ride. The libertarian Cato Institute calls this payback "corporate welfare" and pegs its value at about $80 billion annually; liberal groups estimate its value runs to well over $100 billion each year. No one knows exactly how much money special interests get in return for their campaign contributions, but however much it is, the government "welfare" checks that go to big contributors should be seen for what they are—an income redistribution scheme in which money flows out of taxpayer pockets directly into special interest coffers. The fact that there is a payback for campaign contributions—a financial return on contributors' political donations—is an alarming situation. It is a direct result of the laws that govern the way we fund political elections in this country.

I am not against corporations, businesses, labor unions, and organizations espousing one issue or another trying to influence government. They, like all of us, are affected by public policy and have an interest in persuading elected officials to vote their way. In addition, private enterprise interacts with government in many spheres. Private and public sectors need to work together for the common good. In that light, there are legitimate reasons for government officials and corporate executives and labor leaders to cooperate with each other.

I am not against lobbying either. Lobbyists have a legitimate role in government. Business, labor unions, trade associations, indeed, everyone affected by public policy, should be allowed to state their opinions and contribute their expertise to help shape public policy.

9

But they should do it in an atmosphere uncorrupted by political payola. Merit, not money, should influence political policy decisions. The litmus test for a piece of legislation should be whether or not it furthers the good of the country, not the goals of a campaign contributor. But money, and the power it wields over elected officials, makes a mockery of merit, elevating to power those politicians who are good at fund-raising and those special interests who know what they want from government and are willing to spend whatever it takes to get it.

That's why we need to change the laws governing campaign finance, and that is why I find it outrageous that members of Congress investigating the campaign finance system are more interested in embarrassing their opponents than in fixing the system.

The system needs fixing. The public knows it and so do many politicians. That's why the members of Congress who oppose reform are using investigations as a stalling tactic. Politicians who gained power by raising more money than their opponents are not going to want a system that will give future opponents a fair shot at unseating them.

Because incumbent politicians will not support a system that creates a level playing field for themselves and their opponents, it is up to us—"We, the people"—to get money out of politics.

I left Congress in 1986 to run for governor of Hawaii, and I left with a feeling of having accomplished very little. My experience in Washington showed me that members of Congress are too tied to the system and too dependent on campaign contributions to solve the problem and clean it up themselves. If, as a congressman, I had said what I am saying now, I would have been ostracized by the leadership and powerless to bring anything home for my district. The only way to get anything done in Congress, as I found out, is to accept its rules and play along.

I now wish I had been more outspoken as a congressman in expressing my criticism of the campaign finance system, but it was not a high profile issue at the time. Except for Common Cause, no organization was pushing for reform and until recently, no one could mobilize much public interest. Moreover, except for a handful of notable muckrakers—Elizabeth Drew, who wrote "Washington Report" for *The New Yorker* magazine; Brooks Jackson, then with the *Wall Street Journal*; and Philip Stern, who wrote *The Best Congress Money Can Buy*—few print or broadcast reporters and editors were interested.

This, of course, has changed. The corrupting influence of the current system is well known. New scandals surface almost every day. Names are named. Corruption is exposed. Our leaders drone on about the problems of campaign finance but, instead of seeking solutions, use the issue to blame their opponents. What gets done to change things? Nothing! The lesson is clear: Individual members of Congress will not reform the system until the public demands it. I have said that big money has devalued the power of the individual vote, but there is still plenty of power in the ultimate tally. The system will change when voters get behind the work of reformers.

I have seen how and why Congress maintains a flawed system. What I have seen has also given me insight into how to repair the flaws and reform the system. Members of Congress thrive on routine and tradition. They have no incentive to change the system that brought them power. On the other hand, they are sensitive to public opinion and to their place in history. They will muster political will when voters show political will and demand that things change.

Change is an intrinsic part of the American political system. The system created by our country's founders had many flaws, including slavery and the disenfranchisement of men without property, people of color, and all women. Perceiving their own imperfections, our founders included a built-in mechanism to reform the problems they knew would become evident as the country evolved. Through the civil liberties guaranteed by the Bill of Rights and in the principle of democratic elections, the country's founders institutionalized mechanisms for change. They built in a bias toward reform.

"I do not think we are more inspired, have more wisdom, or possess more virtue than those who will come after us," George Washington

11

wrote. He hoped that future generations endowed with "the advantage of experience" would improve on the work done in his day.

The kind of change I am envisioning never comes easily, especially in an electoral democracy like ours, so tarnished by money. Thomas Paine, whose writings so inspired the American Revolution, had it right when he wrote, "A long habit of not thinking a thing wrong gives it a superficial appearance of being right, and raises at first a formidable outcry in defense of custom."

Pundits and politicians mesmerized by habit continue to defend the current system, but people are starting to wake up. It is ballots, not dollars, that should be the determinant of success in American politics.

Getting Congress to move will not take a majority, at least at first. The process can begin with a minority, a small group with intelligence, energy, and enthusiasm that can convince the critical mass that change is necessary. I believe that there are enough concerned people out there right now to begin the process of change. They can lead the fight for transforming the way we finance our campaign system. My hope is that this book will inspire still more people to take up the mission.

For many years I have wanted to write this book, to use my own congressional experience as a call to action for campaign finance reform. Changing the course of government is an awesome task. But now, finally, we have reached the right moment to turn the public debate into a popular outcry. This book is a call to action, a plea for citizen involvement. We, the people, must back members of Congress—who are supposed to be working for us—into a corner and insist that politicians stop taking and spending money that comes with strings attached because that money empowers special interests and effectively disenfranchises the overwhelming majority of voters. This book is my way of helping to build the momentum.

CHAPTER TWO

Clean Money Campaign Reform

Allow me to "cut to the chase." The American people know there's a problem with the way we pay for campaigns in this country; virtually every opinion poll on the subject in the past year has provided overwhelming evidence of this. We can and should continue to examine the problem and become even more outraged, but I believe it's best to get to the real point: *Let's fix the system.*

I believe an electoral system that is worthy of our country must

1. limit campaign spending and the amount of time candidates spend campaigning;

2. eliminate money as the determinant of a person's political opportunity, access, and influence. Character, integrity, honesty—these are some of the traits that should determine a person's success in politics. Wealth, or access to wealth, should not be the defining factor it currently is;

3. create a financially level playing field so all qualified candidates have access to equal financial resources to conduct competitive campaigns;

4. break the hold monied interests have over the electoral and leg-islative processes of government;

5. be comprehensive and free of loopholes, be easy to understand, and be easy to enforce.

At the same time, such a system must be realistic. Elections cost money. Candidates need money to get their message out to the people. The question is, Who is to finance the candidates' costs?

There are only two ways to pay for elections. One way is to do as we do now and let private interests such as corporations, labor unions, and wealthy individuals continue to foot the bill for democracy. The result, as we know, is the corruption of our political system. Monied interests do not support candidates out of a love of democracy. They support candidates because they want something in return. They want privileged access—a euphemism for special favors that end up costing taxpayers billions of dollars.

The other way to pay for elections is to assume responsibility ourselves. The cost of elections has to be seen as an ordinary cost of living in a democracy. Just as citizens pay for police and fire protection, children's education, our roads, highways, and national security, we ought to be willing to kick in a small amount of money to buy back our electoral system. Studies show that for federal elections—for Congress and the presidency—$6.50 per citizen per year is all it would take to own our democracy. Two or three dollars would do the trick for state elections.

The choice is simple. Either our elected officials work for us or they work for the special interests that provide them with campaign money. Either we keep the status quo and continue to allow a small minority of monied interests to own our political system or we buy it back through a system of full public financing that I will now describe as Clean Money Campaign Reform.

The way I look at the Clean Money option is that it is an investment. We allocate our $5 to a special Democracy Fund and in return get to make demands on the candidates. Those candidates who want to run campaigns with public financing must agree to these demands: a shorter campaign season, limits on the amount they can raise and spend during an election season, and public appearances in debates and other formatted media opportunities. Most importantly, they *must agree not to accept money from special interest contributors.*

Here's how the system would work:

Under the Clean Money option, qualified candidates, regardless of personal wealth, would be able to run for office with the same financial resources—and the same access to the media—as candidates with close ties to big money. Eligibility can be made as tough as the public desires. One idea is this: to become eligible for public financing, candidates would have to raise a specified number of small contributions, perhaps in amounts no greater than $5 or $10. The principle here would be for a candidate to show proof of popular support and not, as is now the case, the ability to hit up fat cats and political action committees for large campaign contributions.

To finance the effort of raising enough qualifying contributions, candidates would need a limited amount of start-up "seed money." They would be allowed to raise that seed money in contributions of up to $100 from private sources. Thus, people who want to put money behind their favorite candidates could do it when it counted—before the election—to help their candidates qualify for public financing, i.e., clean money.

Once the formal campaign season starts, no private money could be spent and fund-raising from private sources would be prohibited. Candidates who prove their popular support by collecting the required number of small qualifying contributions would receive public financing to run in the primary. Winners of primary elections would receive public financing for the general election. Candidates of third or new parties who prove their popular support would be subject to the same rules, regulations, and opportunities as major-party candidates. Special provisions would be made to qualify independent candidates for public financing.

The amount of money candidates receive would be sufficient for effective campaigning. Candidates now spend up to 30 percent of the money they raise from private sources to pay the expenses of further fund-raising. Because candidates who accept clean money are prohibited from raising private money (except for the small amount of start-up seed money and the qualifying contributions) they will not need money for fund-raising costs—a considerable savings on the cost of campaigning right there!

There is an easy way to monitor campaign spending and enforce the Clean Money system. Instead of giving candidates actual money, the Clean Money option would provide them with a line of credit and a special credit or debit card to pay for all major campaign costs. Once a candidate's credit runs out, a candidate would not be able to spend any more money. In other words, candidates would have to limit their spending and keep within a budget. Campaigning within the parameters of a fixed budget would, I believe, be great practice for candidates seeking the power to spend the public's money. It's a provision that should delight fiscal conservatives. Any candidate who can't conduct an election campaign within a fixed budget is not, to my mind, qualified to hold elective office. Under the Clean Money option, a candidate who can't keep within a budget would run out of money before the end of the campaign and likely (and deservingly) lose the election.

To be constitutional, Clean Money Campaign Reform would have to be voluntary. Candidates would be free to opt out of the Clean Money system and raise private money but with tight restrictions. Because of the unfortunate Supreme Court decision, *Buckley v. Valeo*, wealthy candidates who so chose would, as now, be able to spend their own money, but there would be strong incentives to accept public financing. Complying candidates would receive free and discounted media time, which broadcast outlets would provide as a condition of obtaining and retaining their public licenses, as well as matching funds (in the form of additional credit) to counter any excessive spending by their noncomplying opponents.

As former Senator Bill Bradley (D-NJ) has remarked, "A poor man's soapbox does not equal a rich man's wallet." The thrust of the Clean Money Campaign Reform is to create a situation in which all candidates have an equal opportunity to make their case before the public.

This is where what campaign reformers call "free media" comes into play. Under the Clean Money Campaign Reform system, candidates with the proven popular support to qualify for public financing would not have to pay for broadcast advertising but would instead be given a specified amount of free time on radio and/or television to make their case before the people. The broadcast industry may not like this idea, but as a broadcaster myself, I know that we can afford it. Besides, providing some free time in support of democracy is a small return for what the broadcasters currently get—free use of the public airwaves.

No one owns the airwaves. Not NBC or CBS, not Rupert Murdoch or Ted Turner. Nor Cecil Heftel, though I did own a network of Spanish-language radio stations. According to the Radio Act of 1927, broadcast licensees were specifically required to uphold the "public interest, convenience and necessity." In other words, while broadcasters could use the public airwaves free of charge, they were required to operate within rules and regulations formulated by Congress.

The phrase "public interest, convenience and necessity" was not intended to be legal rhetoric. Repeated again in Section 301(a) of the Communications Act of 1934, it asserts government ownership of the airwaves and says that licensees may use—but never own—the airwaves. Broadcasters have a hybrid status: they possess private rights but public responsibilities.

In the 1971 Campaign Finance Reform Act, Congress amended the Communications Act of 1934 by adding, in Section 313(a)7, the doctrine of reasonable access. It held that broadcasters must fulfill the public trust by making time available—free or for money—to all federal candidates. This provision was upheld in 1981,

17

in *CBS v. FCC,* when the Supreme Court gave the priority to the First Amendment rights of candidates and the public to use the public airwaves over the First Amendment right of the broadcaster to deny candidates time.

If the public, through its ownership of the airwaves, is going to provide candidates free time on radio and television, then the public has a right to make demands about how this time is used. Obviously, the First Amendment guarantees candidates the right to say anything they want—and we must never infringe on this most sacred right. We, however, can insist on the format of political advertising. I would suggest that as payment for the use of the public airwaves, political advertising should focus on the candidate and the candidate's message and not, as is so often the case now, on the creative talents of the production experts who produce most television advertising. Thus, in order to make use of free media, candidates themselves would have to be on screen during their political advertisements, speaking in their own voices and not using silken-voiced actors to speak for them.

Candidates who choose the Clean Money option and prove themselves eligible for free media and public financing would also be required to take part in televised debates or other joint appearances. To get the public money, we could also require appearances in different media formats: phone-in shows, interviews, public discussions. Again, the idea is to promote substance over image and to increase the number of times candidates appear on television. With many opportunities to present or defend their positions, a slip of the tongue in one debate would no longer be a decisive factor in the outcome of an election. Just as we are not electing an advertising team, we should not be electing someone with great debating skills (or a good scriptwriter) and little else.

An electoral system that encourages candidates to inform the public must expand, not restrict, the opportunities for communication. To this end, I would encourage the publication of Voter Information Guides to provide every voter basic facts about the candidates. The guides would include biographical material about each candidate, as well as statements by the candidates on their philosophies, goals, reasons for running, and positions on issues. The candidates themselves—not some anonymous election official—would provide the written content. The post office, which has the resources to deliver mail to the occupants of every household in the country, could easily distribute voter information packets a week before the primary and general election.

Another idea to improve the substance of political campaigns came from former Senator and Republican presidential candidate Barry Goldwater. In 1963, Goldwater proposed that he and Jack Kennedy tour the country together as presidential candidates, making joint appearances and debating each other every day. This sort of ongoing debate—not media advertisements—would comprise the guts of a campaign. Kennedy, at least according to Goldwater's autobiography, was intrigued by the idea.

I call Goldwater's idea the "Goldwater Gambit." Here is one way it could work: while campaigning, candidates would travel together for specified times each week. During the day, they might go out on their own, shaking hands on Main Street, talking at a senior center or to a group of high school students, greeting workers at a factory gate, meeting with their own active supporters. Every night, however, they would appear together for a public debate or moderated forum.

The public is tired of candidates who exist as slick advertising creations. We want candidates who talk straight and have the courage of their convictions: a Goldwater or a Truman, for example. Touring together would discourage negative campaigns. It is easy to lie about an opponent from the safety of a television advertisement, especially when a professional actor is reading from a script written by a professional political consultant. It is much harder to falsely attack an opponent face to face.

A campaign that incorporated Goldwater's vision for regular debate would create excitement and involve the public. Democracy is a vibrant institution. To make democracy work, we need to take it away from the interest groups who manipulate it to their advantage. To make democracy work, we need to be creative and audacious.

Clean Money Campaign Reform is a simple, comprehensive way of tackling the major problems of corruption in politics. For about $6.50 a year—less than the price of a night at the movies, a burger and fries, or a drink and a slice of pizza and far less than the current corruption is costing us—we can make it work.

The Clean Money idea is not a pie-in-the-sky abstraction. The states have always been laboratories of democracy, and I predict that's where momentum for the Clean Money reform will build. Already in the 1996 election, voters in Maine, fed up with the legislature's refusal to deal with the corruptive influence of money in their state politics, drafted a ballot initiative called the Maine Clean Elections Act. The initiative, based on the Clean Money model, provided public financing for candidates who agreed not to raise or spend any private money during a specified campaign season. It passed by a vote of 56 percent to 44 percent and proved, I believe, that people are willing to pay a couple of dollars to buy back their electoral system.

There is an old saying that "As Maine goes, so goes the nation." Will the Clean Money Campaign Reform model take off? In June 1997, the Vermont legislature passed a bill similar to the Maine initiative model. In at least ten other states, coalitions have been formed to promote Clean Money Campaign Reform. If we all become involved, a rising tide of citizen anger about the current system and enthusiasm for meaningful reform will carry our fight to Congress.

To be sure, a victory in Congress will not be easy. Monied interests do not want a level playing field that wipes out their special privileges. They will resist reform with everything that they have, which, of course, means money. Once Clean Money is on the political agenda, we can expect the special interests to flood the airwaves with disinformation about campaign finance reform. It will be a real battle to achieve, but the goal of fair and clean elections will be worth it.

Critics of reform will call the Clean Money option "welfare for politicians." In fact, such a plan—a system of alternative, voluntary, full public financing in which candidates who want to take part agree not to raise private money—represents the very opposite of what critics call it. Candidates today are already on a welfare program that is financed by the very same interest groups they are supposed to regulate through legislation. Under the Clean Money option candidates will still get money—but this time from the taxpaying public, who, providing the money, will be the boss. Instead of running filet mignon campaigns compliments of the rich and the powerful, candidates will be forced to run pizza, hamburger, and spaghetti campaigns compliments of the American public.

Public opinion polls consistently confirm that Americans believe the current campaign finance system is corrupt. According to nationwide bipartisan public opinion polls conducted in 1995 by the Gallup organization,

- 92 percent of all Americans believe special-interest contributions buy votes of members of Congress,
- 90 percent say we need to reform the way campaigns are financed to make the politicians accountable to average citizens,
- 88 percent believe those who make large campaign contributions get special favors from politicians,
- and nearly half of all registered voters believe lobbyists and special interests *control* the government in Washington.

Similar polls in August 1996 showed much the same:
- Nearly 70 percent of respondents voiced support for a specific public financing proposal that eliminates private campaign contributions, sets spending limits, and provides candidates who meet a minimum threshold of public support with public funds. The proposal was modeled after an initiative passed by the voters in the state of Maine.
- The support for public financing was strongly bipartisan and demographically diverse. Republicans and self-described "conservatives" approved of the proposal by a 2-to-1 ratio.

21

A 1997 Center for Responsive Politics poll showed

- 66 percent of respondents believe that the influence of political contributions on elections and government policy is a major problem,
- 71 percent said that good people discouraged from running for office by the high cost of campaigns is a major problem,
- 67 percent think their own representatives in Congress would listen to the views of outsiders who made large political contributions before they would listen to constituents' views.

Someday, and I hope it's soon, people will look back on how campaigns were financed in the late twentieth century and will be astounded that people did not go to prison for it. Unless we get real campaign finance reform, future elections are not going to get any better. More money will be spent, fewer people will vote, and the American people will become more alienated and disgusted with the democratic process.

The idea of political change is written into our Constitution. But it's people who make change, it's people who make real the many wonderful ideas written into our Constitution. So I urge all of you reading this book to talk to your friends, your coworkers, and members of your family about the need to reform the system by which we finance our elections. Write letters to the editor about the corrupting influence money has in politics. Send letters, telegrams, faxes, or e-mail messages to your elected representatives when they are shown taking special interest money. Become active in those state organizations promoting Clean Money Campaign Reform. At the end of this book (page 134) is information regarding a petition urging politicians to support Clean Money Campaign Reform. Sign the petition and become politically active. Support and vote for candidates espousing reform. Work against those who refuse to support reform and have financial ties to special interests. Congress will not act unless it feels the heat of grassroots pressure. We must start now.

James Madison, the father of our Constitution, grappled with one of the major questions that spurred me to write this book. "Who are to be the electors of the federal representatives?" he wondered. His answer still strikes a chord today: "Not the rich more than the poor; not the learned more than the ignorant; not the haughty heirs of distinguished names more than the humble sons of obscure and unpropitious fortune." We owe it to our founding fathers to strive to fulfill this vision.

CHAPTER THREE

My Life:
Why I Care So Deeply
about Our Democracy

I am outraged by the country's campaign finance system because I have lived the American dream. I had the opportunity to prosper economically in a way that, in today's political arena, Americans without great financial resources are denied. I believe America is the greatest nation in the world. It is also flawed. America was designed to foster opportunity, promote fairness, and protect people's rights to participate in the political process. The way we currently finance our electoral campaigns undercuts those lofty goals in every way. Our current system of campaign finance denies political opportunity and representation to 99 percent of the people who lack the money to buy access and influence. That infuriates me and I want to do something about it. Some might say I am politically unrealistic, but I believe when the stakes are high we should aim high. I think it is possible to win real reform. I am an optimist.

I was born in Chicago in 1924. When I was five years old, the stock market crashed. My father was in the insurance business, but since no one had enough money to buy insurance during the Great

Depression, we were very poor. We moved constantly from one apartment to another, barely a step ahead of eviction. Everywhere we went and everywhere I looked, I saw people who wanted to work but were instead unemployed and homeless.

Despite our own economic difficulties and the poverty we saw all around us, my parents taught me to believe in our country. They raised me to believe that we are all capable of shaping our own futures and creating our own destinies.

Books were our treasures. Through books I learned how to think clearly, scrutinize issues, and separate faith from facts. My mother, who had a grammar school education, devoured philosophy and history books. She invested me with her knowledge. She taught me about the nobility of Jesus as a great man. She stressed the importance of morality and of embracing religious ethics. She fed me stories about the wisdom of the country's founding fathers. She exposed me to ideas that promoted the sanctity of the United States and its destiny for greatness. She filled me with hope for a better day.

Among my earliest, most cherished memories are those of listening to my mother talking about George Washington, Thomas Jefferson, Thomas Paine, and the other patriots who founded our country, as well as philosophers Ralph Waldo Emerson and Immanuel Kant, among others. She brought them all to life, emphasized the pertinence of their lives, and stressed the power of their ideas about equality, freedom, fairness, and opportunity. The founding fathers are still my heroes, and their ideals represent the core values I have used to guide my life.

My parents taught me that the pursuit of money is not all there is to life. They taught me that the object of life is to serve and to lead and that the highest form of service is to be found as an elected official. Some boys wanted to be baseball stars. I wanted to be a congressman.

President Franklin Delano Roosevelt was my model for a political leader because during the depths of the Depression, he took charge. He did not deny that people were hurting, did not evade reality, but instead took command and resolved to get the economy going again. I remember sitting by the radio and listening to his fireside chats. I did not understand New Deal politics terribly well, but I understood leadership very well. Roosevelt gave me confidence, as he did so many Americans. He taught me the value of facing a problem squarely and honestly. Roosevelt and his advisors analyzed the country's situation and figured out what changes were needed to bring resolution. If one policy did not work, they scrapped it and tried another.

Roosevelt helped me learn how to take action to improve my country. Through him, I realized that if what I believed—that America was the greatest country in the world—did not jibe with what I saw around me—my country falling short of its own ideals—I had to face those facts. I had to work for change and demand better of myself and my country.

That is a long explanation, but it speaks to why I became so bitterly disappointed when I succeeded in politics. I started my political activities in Chicago, in high school, by initiating a student forum that encouraged controversy and debate. In those days, a number of students were active in the Socialist Party. Some even joined Communist cells. That was the 1930s after all, and people were responding in different and sometimes extreme ways to the nation's desperate economic crisis. I did not care—I was horrified to see young idealists rejecting God, religion, and our own American political heritage. I, too, experienced the worst of the Great Depression, but my support of American ideals never wavered.

I became a strong anti-Communist and spearheaded a student group that criticized left-wing groups. I denounced Communists as traitors and spoke out boldly in favor of American values, democracy, freedom, and individual rights. Although I am still a vociferous anti-Communist, I am not as intolerant as I was in high school, thanks to Senator Joseph McCarthy, the low-life redbaiter from Wisconsin.

When he started pointing his finger at everyone with whom he disagreed, accusing them of membership in the Communist Party, I reassessed my own point of view. To my mind, McCarthyism, which denied political opportunity to advocates of unpopular ideas, represented the epitome of anti-Americanism. Speech should be encouraged, not squelched. Individual's rights should be respected regardless of what people do with them. Everyone—rich or poor, left or right—should have the opportunity to participate in the political arena. I may have been a card-carrying hothead in high school, but McCarthyism changed that. While I may still be outspoken, I also have a deep and abiding respect for tolerance and fair-mindedness.

I served in the Army Air Corps during World War II. I wanted to attend officer candidates school and go overseas, but a severe asthma attack disqualified me. I refused an offer of medical discharge and spent the war as a cryptologist.

The federal government did right by its World War II veterans. I was able to attend college and law school under the GI Bill. In college, at Arizona State, I took a year of accounting and found I had a head for business. I started doing bookkeeping for local businesses and learned to appreciate sound business management. It stood me in good stead when I got to Congress, where I was amazed to discover that many of my colleagues had no concept whatsoever of fiscal responsibility.

In the 1950s, television was just becoming popular and I decided that radio represented a great economic opportunity. That might not sound so smart, but it worked out quite well. At the time, new networks were building their audience by hiring radio personalities and giving them television shows. The word on the streets was that radio was dead, and station owners were terrified that their livelihoods were on the brink of disaster. I saw a tremendous opportunity and snapped up stations dirt cheap. I played what people wanted to hear and made the stations immensely popular and profitable.

When I moved to Hawaii, I became active in Democratic politics. In 1976, I decided to seek the Democratic nomination for Congress. As a political newcomer, I was still naive about the power of political machines and the importance of campaign money. That naiveté did not last long.

Because mainland Democrats had championed Hawaiian state-hood, most Hawaiians supported the Democratic Party. I believed state party leaders had become arrogant, corrupt, and bloated by the illusion of power that can come from a multiyear reign. They were in bed with local real estate developers and labor unions, which, at that time in Hawaii, wielded a great deal of political power. I wanted to run against and break the power of the Democratic machine.

Since the Republican Party lacked voter support, I ran as a Democrat in the Democratic primary. As an insurgent Democrat, I was completely frozen out of party fund-raising efforts. No one could afford to offend the party bosses, so no one gave me sizable contributions. The harder I worked for legitimate campaign funding, the more I found myself rebuffed by traditional Democratic contributors. I realized I had to spend my own funds or give up the race. I knew if I used my own money, it would free me from groveling to special interests. Using my own money would also pit me, at least for the moment, firmly against Democratic Party powerhouses. I did some soul searching, decided to fight, and won the primary.

To my great surprise, many local Democratic leaders shifted everything—party money, labor, endorsements—to the Republican candidate, Fred Rohlfing, an insider and long-time member of the state legislature. That cinched my status as an outsider. Even though I ran as a Democrat, I was perceived as thoroughly independent.

By the time the election was over, I had raised $30,000 in small contributions and spent more than $500,000 of my own money. But I had won. I was a congressman.

I did not get there without having plenty of mixed feelings regarding candidates who spend their own money to run for office. Money cannot make a winner out of a candidate the public correctly perceives as a loser. Just look at the failed campaigns of wealthy people like Steve Forbes, a political neophyte who in 1996 ran for president by lending his own campaign more than $37 million, and Michael Huffington, who in 1994 spent $28.4 million to try to buy a Senate seat from California. Had I not been allowed to spend my own

28

money, I could not have mounted an effective campaign against the political bosses. Then again, that means only the very wealthy are in a position to run truly independent campaigns. The inherent unfairness of the situation is not at all lost on me. Even though I believe the people of Hawaii benefitted from my election, as did I, the system is flawed.

The flaw that allowed me to finance my own race is tucked away in a bad U.S. Supreme Court decision, *Buckley v. Valeo*, which was issued in 1976. Let me give you a little history. In 1971, Congress authorized a system of voluntary public financing for presidential elections: the Federal Election Campaign Act. Under this system, candidates who agreed not to spend private money during the general election would receive full campaign funding financed by an optional $1 tax credit check-off on income tax returns (the amount was later increased to $3). Conversely, presidential candidates who wanted to raise money from private sources for campaigning would not receive any public financing.

Fueled by public outrage over Watergate—Richard Nixon's flagrant abuses of democratic rule—reformers in 1974 were able to get Congress to pass a series of bold amendments to the 1971 Federal Election Campaign Act. These amendments created a system of partial public financing for the presidential primary and established for congressional races (1) limits on contributions for individuals and political action committees, (2) spending limits for individual congressional campaigns, (3) overall limits on the amount of money a national party could spend on a candidate's behalf, and (4) limits on what individual contributors could spend on "independent expenditures."[1]

An unlikely coalition of conservatives and liberals, including the New York Civil Liberties Union, immediately challenged the new law

---

1. Independent expenditures are campaign expenditures an individual or political committee makes to advocate one candidate's election or defeat for the benefit of another candidate. To be a legitimate independent expenditure, the candidate and his or her staff may not have any prior knowledge of the advocate's contribution and must not have cooperated or consulted with the contributor.

in the courts. They argued that money spent on an election campaign ought to be seen as free speech, not money.

On January 30, 1976, the Supreme Court returned a split decision known as *Buckley v. Valeo.* It upheld the principle of voluntary public financing for presidential general elections and maintained limits on campaign contributions from individuals and political action committees. The ruling went on to say it was unconstitutional to limit spending for campaigns and independent expenditures. Finally, the decision said it was a violation of free speech to limit the amount of personal money a candidate could spend on his or her own campaign. As a result, I was able to finance my campaign with as much of my own money as I wished. Otherwise, I would have never been elected to Congress.

There is no doubt that *Buckley v. Valeo* gives wealthy people an advantage. It discriminates against candidates who, however well qualified they might otherwise be, do not have deep pockets. It is not fair, but in a system such as we have now, and that we had when I first ran for office, money can make or break a candidate. Candidates either go begging to the established sources of money—and become beholden to their interests—or, if able, use their own money as I did. There are a few members of Congress who are able to raise lots of money from small contributors. But they are the exceptions. Like it or not, personal wealth or access to special interest money is what candidates need to get elected. It's wrong. And that is why I passionately believe we have to change the system.

It would be deceptive of me not to acknowledge that because I used my own money, nobody—Republican or Democrat—was able to run a serious campaign against me. I took full advantage of my situation and was as independent as they come, but I also took my job as a congressman extremely seriously. I earned the support of the people in my district and they re-elected me to Congress four more times, each time with over 80 percent of the vote.

I was always conscious of my privileged position in personally financing my first campaign even though I had limited personal resources. The need to raise money, and what my colleagues had to go through to do it, offended me. Because I had my own financial resources, I did not have to kowtow to anyone. Nor did I have to squander my time going to fund-raising events on Capitol Hill. Sometimes in Washington, I might show up at another member's fund-raiser, but only if I liked that candidate and believed in what he or she was doing.

Campaigning, especially the first time, soured me on the system. Once I arrived in Washington and saw how things worked there, I knew at some point I would have to take real action. I regret that I waited ten years to write this book, although during this last decade the issue of campaign finance has finally become part of the public debate. I applaud those who raised the issue early on, even when it seemed to be going nowhere. The disgust about campaign finance that I felt as a candidate for and a member of Congress has never left me. I've come late to the game, but I'm in it for the duration.

What exasperated me in Washington was that all around me good, decent, hard-working, well-intentioned colleagues were capitulating to the special interests that funded their campaigns. Money ruled—and still rules—the roost in Congress, but a democracy that is driven by money is not a popular democracy.

Clean Money Campaign Reform would give candidates who can prove that they have popular voter support an equal amount of money to run equally competitive campaigns. On a financially level playing field, the real currency would be personal character, leadership abilities, and the merit of one's ideas. Such a playing field would liberate candidates and elected officials from the onerous burden of incessant fund-raising. That, in turn, would give the public a greater choice of candidates. Once elected, lawmakers would no longer be obligated to do favors for their benefactors. Public servants would be free to listen to their constituents.

Democrats: How and Why We Went Wrong

I entered Congress during a momentous shift in the pattern and intensity of campaign financing. Historically, Republicans raised more money than Democrats. Republicans depended on contributions from business interests, although some industries tended to support Democrats for reasons of trade and regional politics. Democrats, on the other hand, primarily depended on money from labor unions.

Even though Republicans raised more money, a couple of things kept Democrats competitive. First, Democrats used their labor contributions to fund get-out-the-vote drives. Second, Democrats could depend on big city political machines to get voters to the polls. So while Republicans had the lion's share of the money, Democrats could count on getting a substantial portion of the vote. If popular mythology is correct, certain big city party bosses could even raise the dead to vote Democratic.

By the mid-1970s, several important factors affecting the traditional balance between Republicans and Democrats began to change. Labor unions began to lose influence in society and over their own members. The Republican's Southern Strategy, instituted by Richard Nixon to blunt the influence of the radical politics of the 1960s, started paying off. Consequently, many white working-class and ethnic voters began voting Republican to protest Democrats' embrace of civil rights and feminism. Big city Democratic machines were also losing ground. Even though the Hawaii Democratic machine, one of the most entrenched, remained powerful during my years in Congress, elsewhere corrupt big city party bosses were being driven from power. Big city political organizations such as New York City's Tammany Hall and the Daley machine in Chicago were being beaten—often by insurgent Democrats running against old guard leaders. This, coupled with the increasing inability of labor to turn out its members for Democrats, presented a crisis for the party.

The election of Ronald Reagan in 1980 brought home the realities of the new politics. While the loss of the White House was terrifying for the Democrats, the loss of congressional seats that year was almost worse: the 1980 Republican landslide swept a dozen Democratic senators out of office. In the House, the GOP picked up a net thirty-three seats. Among the losers in 1980 were a number of colleagues who were considered unbeatable. Representative Al Ullman, chairman of the Ways and Means Committee, John Brademas, the Democratic whip, and James Corman, chairman of the Democratic Congressional Campaign Committee (DCCC) were all conscientious legislators with presumably safe seats. Yet the Reagan landslide drove them out of office.

This was not a happy time for the Democrats. In the aftermath of the 1980 elections, I remember many of my fellow Democrats feeling that Republicans would soon control both houses of Congress and, with their access to corporate money, have a hold that would not be easily shaken. If the Democrats were going to compete on a level playing field with the Republicans, they decided they were going to have to learn how to raise money from the same base of funders that had usually supported the Republican Party.

Tony Coelho, a congressman from California's Central Valley, was one of the first Democrats in Congress to clearly understand that the grassroots approach to voter turnout was no longer working. When he replaced James Corman as chairman of the DCCC, Coelho's mandate could not have been clearer: raise money and help Democrats maintain control of the House of Representatives.

Before Coelho took over, the DCCC amassed most of its cash through an annual $500-a-plate dinner. During the 1980 election cycle, the DCCC raised approximately $2 million. Its rival, the National Republican Congressional Committee, raised $26.8 million. Republicans were feeling their power. Sensing that control of the federal government was within its grasp, the Reagan administration, with support from the U.S. Chamber of Commerce and other political allies, pressured corporate PACs to confine their giving to the Republican Party.

Coelho had his work cut out for him.

I liked Tony Coelho. He was a young guy, hard working, idealistic but pragmatic, a fighter for the public interest. He had huge potential. In California, Coelho successfully located the common ground between agribusiness and the administrators of public water and wetlands projects. He was very popular in his district and could have remained in Congress for as long as he wanted, but he was ambitious. He took over the DCCC, and in my judgment, he did that without ulterior motives. He simply wanted to keep the Democrats in power so they could pursue his vision of what it meant to have private and public sectors working together for the good of the country.

In his determination to raise money, Coelho turned to the corporate sector. Soon after he became the DCCC chairman, Coelho started promoting Democratic candidates to business groups. Coelho understood that corporate PACs were fundamentally practical, not ideological, and his approach proved it. He would explain that the Democrats were the party in power and that if business groups wanted to work with the Democrats, business groups would have to give Democrats the same kind of support they had traditionally given Republicans.

Coelho's message fell on receptive ears. The corporate PACs appreciated that for the first time in history, Democrats were actively courting them. In his wonderful book about Coelho's courtship of business money, *Honest Graft*, Brooks Jackson wrote, "As a group, they [the corporate PACs] remained far more interested in currying favor with the ruling faction than in promoting the free-market ideology the Republicans championed." Coelho's pragmatism impressed many corporate leaders. What a coup it would be if the Democrats, like the Republicans, became the party for business.

Coelho knew the Hill (which is what insiders call Congress) and he knew money made the system go. A man of exceptional energy, he was constantly organizing fund-raising events that brought congressional Democrats together with corporate leaders, lobbyists, and people who had money. He knew I used my own money to run my campaigns, but he constantly pressed me to go to his fund-raisers, if only to represent the party and convince lobbyists that the Democratic Party was worth supporting.

Coelho was as imaginative as he was persistent in his efforts to raise money. He initiated railroad trips and scenic outings to enable corporate lobbyists to network informally with members of Congress. He took over the posh Greenbrier Hotel in West Virginia and invited lobbyists to spend a weekend playing golf with party leaders.

He had the skills of a social director at a singles mixer. At candidate forums and at fund-raising cocktail parties, he paraded prospective Democratic candidates before lobbyists and PAC officials as if the candidates were debutantes at a coming-out party. Lobbyists called these events "cattle calls" and "meat markets." Everyone wore nametags, and Coelho would promote candidates as moderates who could be depended upon to cooperate with the needs of business.

Coelho's fund-raisers were social events, real love-fests. Everyone seemed to be everyone else's friend. As far as I could tell, no one asked for favors, but contacts were made. It was all very subtle, very clean. Slick, but not crass. Most people, after all, love to be courted. Later, lobbyists would call a member's office and ask for a meeting. Even at the meeting, lobbyists would not blatantly ask for a favor. On the contrary, they would try to be helpful to the lawmaker by offering to help get legislative support for bills in which members were interested or that affected the member's district. That was their come-on: to ask what the member needed.

There are 435 representatives (and 100 senators) in Congress and no one knows everyone. Lobbyists take it upon themselves to advocate for those who cooperate with them. In many ways, they are the glue, or the spider's web, of the political process. A good lobbyist knows how to network and works diligently to bring what one member wants to the attention of other members. Lobbyists who use money to gain access spread their influence around with good will. They build social capital and obligate members. Lobbyists' purpose, though, is not to serve the members they befriend but to serve the clients who pay their salaries. Always. Lobbyists are fluent and persistent. Everything they do is oriented toward that one definitive moment when they ask for payback, the moment they call in their chits.

Members cannot cover all the issues personally. Lobbyists present themselves as resource people on issues of interest. They can be quite helpful; they have a lot of information, a lot of educational material, and they are only too happy to offer their resources to members. Yet it's clear that their material is totally one-sided; it does not, I believe, jibe with the realities of public policy.

There are arguments to be made pro and con on most public issues. The role of the legislator is to listen to competing arguments and determine which side of an issue best advances public policy. But the way lobbyists present an issue, there is no gray area or ambiguity between what is right and what is wrong. Their side is the only right side; if lobbyists had their way—and campaign contributions are meant to assure that they get their way—alternative arguments would have no place in a debate.

The more I dealt with lobbyists, the more disgusted I became. They have no conscience about America or concern for the people of America. The only thing they know besides their issue is who pays them and what they have to achieve to earn their money. Their purpose in life is winning legislative favors for their clients. The country, the people, be damned.

Tony Coelho not only brought Democratic members together with lobbyists but also provided a direct link for members of Congress to the corporate leaders who hired lobbyists—the wealthy individuals with money to give. One of Coelho's most successful money-raising gambits was the "Speaker's Club." Membership cost $5,000 a year for an individual and $15,000 for a PAC. The DCCC promised that Speaker's Club members would "serve as trusted, informal advisors to the Democratic Members of Congress." The DCCC also promised that club members would "gain valuable information" during "exclusive" briefings on tax, budget, and regulatory matters. The Speaker's Club was the equivalent of the Republican National Committee's Eagle Club. Both organizations existed to woo corporate donors by selling access to party leaders.

On Wall Street, profiting from nonpublic "inside" information is a criminal offense. Stocktraders have gone to jail for inside trading. The Securities and Exchange Commission prohibits brokers from using inside information for personal profit. But when the Democratic Party began trading information for money, and when business leaders began giving money to Democratic legislators in order to promote public policies that would enhance their profits, no one batted an eye. The Republicans, after all, were doing the same thing. And the practice continues—but with one important difference. The media and a growing number of campaign reformers do more than bat an eye in the face of political insider trading. We now cry "corruption" and demand reform. Yet the practice continues. The wealthy elite and compliant politicians treat representative government as if it were an exclusive, private club.

Another venue Coelho explored for funding was soft money.[1] Before Coelho, the DCCC did not attempt to raise soft money, but in his scramble to catch up with the Republicans, Coelho was drawn to this possibility. In 1985, he wrote a revealing memo to the DCCC

---

1. Soft money is political money raised by national and state parties that is *not regulated* by federal campaign finance law because, in theory, it is for generic "party building" activities such as getting out the vote. In practice, it is often used to benefit specific federal candidates, and thus it has become a major vehicle for skirting the limitations and restrictions of federal law. In 1992, the national parties raised $83 million in soft money and an estimated $205 million more was raised by state parties. Much of this money came in contributions of $50,000 and $100,000.

about the uses of soft money. "The DCCC has pushed hard on soft money because the DCCC believes that it is one of the principal ways the DCCC can accelerate the catch-up process with the Republicans," wrote Coelho. "There is simply not enough hard money to do everything that the DCCC would like to do.[2] Moreover, it would be foolish to spend hard money that could be used in support of candidates on projects that can be legitimately paid for with soft money."

Coelho's success at raising soft money financed construction of the Democratic National Headquarters. And when television networks refused to give the party free time to respond to President Reagan's State of the Union Address (the networks argued that Reagan was speaking as president of all the people, not as a partisan Republican), the Democrats used soft money to buy network time for their answer.

Virtually single-handedly, Coelho created a successful fundraising apparatus that thwarted Republican attempts to monopolize business and corporate money. In 1982, we Democrats picked up twenty-six House seats. In 1984, despite Reagan's landslide victory, we lost only fifteen seats and maintained our hold on the House. In 1986, the last time I ran for Congress, we picked up five House seats and seven Senate seats and seemingly solidified our congressional majority. The remarkable resilience and popularity of the Republican president was not enough to give his party control of Congress.

In one light, Coelho had done nothing more than replicate traditional Republican fund-raising efforts. The GOP traditionally offered its big donors insider privileges, and that is what we Democrats now did. But then again, Republicans prided themselves as being the party of big business. Under Tony Coelho, my party, supposedly the party of the people, sold itself to monied Republican contributors. When the money was counted after the 1986 election, PACs had given $87.4 million to House candidates, and Democrats

---

2. Hard money is *federally regulated* campaign contributions and other monies spent for the purpose of influencing the outcome of a federal election. This is money generally given directly to campaigns or candidates.

got 63 percent of that. House Democratic incumbents who ran for re-election in 1986 realized $41 million from PACs; Republican incumbents received $25 million.

Coelho succeeded at raising funds, but at what cost to the party's soul? In 1989, Robert B. Reich, the future secretary of labor in the Clinton administration, wrote an op-ed piece in *The New York Times* bemoaning the Democrats' loss of direction. Democratic leaders "convinced big business and Wall Street it was smarter to back incumbent Democrats than aspiring Republicans," he wrote but added that "it is difficult to represent the little fellow when the big fellow pays the tab."

In another light, Coelho's fund-raising success caused a split between the party professionals whose principal concern was maintaining control of Congress and the party's activist rank and file whose concern was asserting the party's traditional liberal ideology. The populist policies that excited grassroots activists were often repugnant to the business-oriented contributors providing dollars to keep the party in power. And the price the party paid to win business backing was repugnant to the partisans who wanted to keep the Democrats a party of the working and middle classes. The more disenchanted party activists became with Democratic incumbents' pro-business policies, the less the party could depend on them to work for its candidates,

The cycle was self-perpetuating. As the Democrats' activist base dried up, the party became more dependent on television to get out its message. That meant raising money to buy advertising time and tailoring party policies to the business groups that had the money. The more money the party raised, the more disillusioned liberal activists became. In 1988, columnist Robert Kuttner wrote in *The American Prospect* magazine that Democratic Party "campaigns are financed in large part by the very people populists must challenge."

I never had to sell myself as a politician with whom special interests could do business because I was able to finance my campaigns with my own money. I escaped the indignities of the "meat markets" and "cattle calls." More than most members of Congress, I was able to balance the needs of my own district with my sense of national priorities and vote my conscience rather than vote to appeal to my cash constituents.

Although there are a few members of Congress who love fund-raising and who love the glad-handing that goes with it, I am sure most would love to be relieved of that burden. Still, very few will go the route of unilateral disarmament and foreswear all fund-raising. All politicians who want to serve in elective office, including the most conscientious members of Congress, are trapped by the system. They are unable to make a break from the demands of raising money, no matter what it costs their constituents, their consciences, and their desire to do good.

Democrats were the self-proclaimed party of the "little people" during the periods of the New Deal and the Great Society when their domestic policies had great success. Were Democrats to reverse course and once again promote class-based politics, they might regain their soul. Indeed, turning back to their populist roots and rebuilding their moral base by promoting an end to money politics could be the Democrats' salvation. They haven't as much to lose, money-wise. With the power shift and GOP takeover after the 1994 congressional elections, contributions from business and industry began moving back to the Republicans anyway.

The role of money continues to expand in American politics. Because of the ever-increasing importance of television advertisements, it takes more money to compete in elections than it did when I was running for office, and that means more pressure on candidates to raise money. The more money candidates need to raise, the more beholden they become to the interests who finance their elections.

While the magnitude of fund-raising has increased, the dynamics that shape corruption have not changed. The Democratic Party seems as compromised with a Democrat in the White House as it was when a Republican controlled it. In *Locked in the Cabinet,* the memoir Robert Reich wrote about his tenure as secretary of labor, Reich quotes Representative Martin Sabo (D-MN), who despaired, "We're owned by them. Business. That's where the campaign money comes from now. In the 1980s we gave up on the little guys."

40

CHAPTER FIVE

Campaign Contributions and the Budget Deficit

I entered Congress determined to tackle the budget deficit. Toward the end of my first term, I decided to join the House Ways and Means Committee—which deals with issues of government taxation and, by extension, government spending—so I could fight what I saw as a squandering of taxpayer money. Getting on the committee was harder than I expected. Since I was not part of any geographic bloc or philosophic camp, there was no particular group in the House to rally support for me. I had to make my case on my own.

To bolster that case, I wrote a letter to each of the Democratic committee members. In my letter, I described my belief that we needed to reform the tax system, which I called unfair and corrupt. I wrote that lobbyists' dollars have too much influence in drafting tax legislation, that money buys tax favors for those who give it. Money carries too much weight with members of the Ways and Means Committee, I wrote, especially with committee and subcommittee chairmen who get most of the campaign contributions.

When I wrote that letter I was new in Congress. I based it on my gut instinct as much as hard knowledge. In retrospect, I underestimated the influence of money. I thought that campaign contributions *influenced* tax legislation; I now believe it *determines* tax legislation. Tax breaks are the return on investment interest groups get for campaign contributions.

My effort, which didn't endear me to the party leadership, inspired the first contested election for a committee assignment in the Democratic caucus. At least two committee seats were open. The House leadership tried to rally support behind their designated candidates, but even as an outsider, I remained in the running. Ballot after ballot failed to achieve the necessary majority. In the end, I finished second to Representative Thomas Downey of New York and so, with Downey, won a seat on the committee.

Members of Congress treat the budget deficit in much the same way they treat campaign contributions. They simply redefine the terms to justify a practice that would be considered scandalous—if not criminal—in other areas of society and unacceptable to reasonable people. In the congressional world of campaign finance, bribery is called a "campaign contribution" and fiscal irresponsibility is neutralized by the term "deficit spending."

Remarkably, Congress ignores all principles of elementary accounting in writing a budget. What comes in as revenue through taxes is supposed to balance with what goes out as spending. That is a basic principle that even advocates of "deficit spending" used to understand. The great English economist, John Maynard Keynes, for example, advocated deficit spending as a means of lifting the economy out of the Great Depression of the 1930s. But Keynes also suggested that when the economy was booming, excess revenue be saved in order to finance the recovery out of the next economic downturn. In other words, savings from the "good times" would be used to increase government spending during the "bad times" when the private sector, as happens cyclically, would be unable to provide people with good-paying jobs.

It is unfortunate that in today's demagogic political climate where television sound bites drown out reasoned discussion, the idea of a balanced budget has become so highly partisan. Those who advocate cutting spending are blamed for opposing social programs. Others who advocate retaining certain programs are criticized for wanting to perpetuate dependence on entitlements. Some, dare I say it, seem to want to retain certain types of spending so that their special interest campaign contributors can continue to benefit. It's all a contest to blame and embarrass political opponents and has little to do with the public interest, the national good. That's unconscionable.

The argument for a balanced budget should be based only on what is best for the country. Catering to special interests—be they business or labor, race or class based—threatens the nation. We should match government spending to the best estimate of government revenue and slash, keep, or create government programs on the basis of merit, on what's good for the country and what's best for the American people.

To me, balancing the budget is not an ideological mantra. It is sound financial management. Every family knows that you cannot spend more than you make. You should not treat a capital expenditure—for a home improvement, a new car, or your child's education—as if it were a daily operating expense, a simple cash flow matter.

The federal budgetary process does not operate under such a constraint. The federal budget makes no distinction between capital and operating expenditures. If the federal government wants to ignore sound bookkeeping principles and spend more money than it takes in, it just raises taxes, floats more bonds, prints more money, or passes the cost of financing the debt on to future generations.

I entered Congress when Jimmy Carter went to the White House. We both wanted to make things better. Like Carter, I was concerned about government spending. At that time, 1977, the total national debt was $706.4 billion, the highest it had ever been (but approximately one-eighth of what it is today). I wanted to balance the budget as a financial principle. But from my first days in office, I was astounded at how easily Congress could spend money that didn't exist.

43

My frustration level reached its limit right away. I began warning colleagues that we could not continue deficit spending on a large scale. We couldn't afford the self-destructive interest rates and inflation rates. We were totally irresponsible in appropriating money for pork-barrel projects that served no national good. I said this in all kinds of ways, and so did a number of other members of Congress, all to no avail.

Those of us who complained had hopes of doing something about the debt problem. After all, we were members of Congress, elected leaders. In reality, however, we were stuck on the sidelines, marginal players. As newcomers in Congress, we hadn't yet proven ourselves to the congressional leaders; we weren't yet part of the system, *their* system, by which they controlled the Congress. The leaders of Congress were not themselves corrupt or evil. They had come up through the ranks (as I had the opportunity to do). They had learned how the system functioned (had mastered it enough to rise into positions of power) and saw no reason to shake it up.

Being independent-minded and having learned in business to take a jaundiced view of conventional wisdom, I was not one to passively follow their lead. The people of Hawaii had elected me to Congress to represent them, not to close my eyes and accept the platitudes of the existing leadership. One of the first things I observed—how could I help but observe this, it stood out so obviously—was that money drives the system and that the system, at least as it operates through the mechanism of the House Committee on Ways and Means—enacts tax benefits favored by interest groups who give campaign contributions to the members of Ways and Means. I also learned quickly that those who oppose irresponsible spending have to be willing to buck the system. And to buck the system is to risk compromising the influence—or the potential influence—one has by dint of being a member of Congress.

As a candidate for president in 1976, Jimmy Carter had promised to cut wasteful spending. One of his first acts, within a month after he took office, was to buck the congressional leadership by proposing the elimination of nineteen of the thirty-two water projects Congress had approved for the western states. Most of these projects were boondoggles—everyone knew that—and Carter was right to oppose them. But the projects had very powerful supporters in Congress.

I knew Carter was absolutely correct in opposing these expensive water projects. They should have been abandoned or never have been started. I had given my commitment to Speaker Tip O'Neill and the house leadership before analyzing the projects and coming to the conclusion that President Carter was correct. But based on my knowledge of how the Congress operated, it would have alienated me from the congressional leaders if I had reneged on my verbal commitments.

I am not proud of my vote opposing President Carter on the water diversion projects. But it was a lesson for me about the role that big money plays in the decisions of Congress. Jimmy Carter had the background to understand technological issues, and he had a long history of questioning the value of water diversion projects. When the projects came up for funding in 1977, he wrote a letter to Congress pointing out some of the problems they posed:

- California's Auburn-Folsom Dam, for example, designed to channel water into California's agribusiness heartland, the Central Valley, was going to be built in an earthquake zone. Thousands of people living downstream would be in potential jeopardy.

- North Dakota's Garrison irrigation project affected water flow in many of Canada's important western rivers. For this reason, Canada opposed the project as a violation of an international treaty that protected rivers and waterways flowing through both countries.

- Louisiana's Atchafalaya River navigation project, which would have widened a waterway at taxpayer expense, benefitted a very few private companies.

45

- The Central Arizona project and four other projects in the Colorado River Basin would have worsened water shortages and salinity concentrations in the Colorado River.

When Carter publicly attacked these boondoggles, Congress generally felt that he was—to use Senator Edmund Muskie's words—treating the Congress like the Georgia legislature. Senator Henry "Scoop" Jackson commented that "The Administration does not understand that the Congress had grown more independent and stronger as the natural fallout of Watergate. . . . The Senate, in case you had not noticed, is a pretty powerful body these days." But the issue was neither congressional sensitivity nor senatorial prerogatives. It was money. As Dan Beard, then a veteran environmental lobbyist and now senior vice president of the Audubon Society, told investigative reporter Robert Schlesinger, "Every . . . natural resource issue that affects the western United States really is a debate not about the merits of how we should manage these resources, but a debate about how much in the way of subsidies people receive."

Referring to the water diversion projects irrigating California's Central Valley, Beard told Schlesinger, "It's all being piped at federal expense—and that really means taxpayer expense. These are very wealthy people who have done very well, and they don't hesitate to pay campaign contributions and use other influence to keep this subsidy flowing."

One day while I was on the House floor, I was called to the cloakroom to take a phone call from President Carter. This was my first conversation with him. He wanted my vote on the western water bill. I told him I couldn't support him. I told him that, unfortunately, I had already made a commitment to the House leadership. Perhaps he could tell I didn't have my heart in rejecting his plea, as he cajoled and pressed me on the issue for about twenty minutes.

Merit was on Jimmy Carter's side. Big money was on the projects' side. In order to keep the money flowing into Democratic party coffers, Speaker O'Neill pressured me to vote with the party. *Money talked to the leadership and I voted wrong.* (Carter ultimately succeeded in forcing members of Congress to cut half of the projects that they wanted. But the Central Arizona and the Garrison projects were eventually completed, and there are still public works and agribusiness interest groups promoting the Auburn-Folsom Dam construction.)

There I had been, a lowly freshman. I had resisted the president of the United States—my own party's president. He could have talked until he was blue in the face and I still would have resisted him—why and for what? I agreed with his opposition to the western water bill. I agreed with him 100 percent!

In Congress, the system is based on following the leaders: the speaker, the party whips, and the heads of the various committees and subcommittees. And following their leadership almost always means voting to spend money. I knew that if I bucked the party leaders on the spending bills that they wanted, I could expect to get no assistance from them in passing the bills that I wanted. If I didn't play by the rules of their game, I would be sitting on the bench for the rest of my time in Congress—with no influence at all.

The government spends hundreds of billions of dollars each year that are of no benefit to 99 percent of the American people. Those water projects were important not for the general well-being of the public but for interest groups that had a financial stake in their construction. The vote on the water projects was typical of what members of Congress vote on during the years they spend in Congress. The system is all-powerful. And the system is manipulated for the private interests of those with the money to fund election campaigns.

Looking back, I wish that I had supported the president, broken with the Democratic leadership, and established my independence. But I was new to Congress. And the pressures on new members to follow the party line are powerful. The congressional leadership (of both parties) is determined to push forward its legislative agenda. To get a majority behind them, the leaders often have to entice or "bribe" recalcitrant members with appropriations for their congressional districts.

Bribery is the way the system works. Campaign contributors entice, or "bribe," members to advance contributors' interests. Members bribe other members to gain support for legislation favored by the special interests.

Very early on in my congressional career, I was astounded to see how Congress's drive to spend money was independent of—and indeed, completely overwhelmed by—its need to raise tax revenue. During my time in Congress I made many speeches about our becoming a debtor nation. I said we had to bring the debt and the deficits under control. As a freshman member, I did not get much attention from the media or from the congressional leadership. I remember feeling despair that there was no way the leadership or other members of Congress were going to focus on the deficit problem—unless they first focused on our rotten system of financing campaigns.

Congress appropriates money to please campaign contributors and then tries to cut taxes to please them again. Giving away money while cutting taxes is a recipe for disaster. More spending and lower taxes are two ideas that do not mesh. During the Reagan years, the national debt skyrocketed. By the end of the 1980s, it stood at $4 trillion.

Despite all the current talk about balancing the budget, the national debt is still rising at a rate of $594 million per day. The current (1997) wave of prosperity has created increasing tax revenues and a smaller budgetary deficit. Predictably, the cuts in federal spending that have helped to decrease the deficit have come at the expense of those people who don't make large campaign contributions. Large campaign contributors continue to reap their rewards. We continue to spend more to pay interest on the national debt than we do on all domestic programs combined, aside from Social Security. Although the debt has increased more slowly in recent years than it did in the 1980s, by 1997, it had risen to $5.4 trillion.

Five trillion dollars is a lot of money. What did it pay for? Where did it go?

Government services have diminished. Many roads and bridges are dangerously decayed. In some places, water is undrinkable. In many parts of the country, mass transit is nonexistent. Public schools are danger zones. Family farms are going out of business. Urban neighborhoods, and in some cases entire cities, are unsafe—almost unlivable. Although the crime rate now seems to be going down, we've done little to heal the extremes in class division or to deal effectively with the brutality, homelessness, and racial isolation of impoverished inner cities.

The national debt may be the biggest problem we face, but it is only one of myriad disasters Washington has brought us in recent years. The consequences of public policies designed to appease political funders rather than to meet the needs of a changing society have been costly—and not just in squandered lives and wasted opportunity. For years, Washington threw money at ill-conceived welfare programs that created a numb and violence-prone underclass, rural and urban. Welfare encouraged dependency, not responsibility.

The same can be said of the system that some have called "corporate welfare." Congress continues to return huge subsidy programs and other "entitlements" on investments made by some of its most faithful campaign contributors. An appalling example of this came during my years on Capitol Hill.

Representative Fernan St Germain (D-RI) was chairman of the House Banking, Finance and Urban Affairs Committee and the author of legislation that would deregulate the savings and loan (S&L) industry. From my vantage point on the Ways and Means Committee, I could see in advance that there were going to be problems with deregulation. Well before the bill was voted on, I tried to bring up the subject with St Germain.

One day, while seated next to St Germain in the House cloakroom, I made the approach. "Fred," I started out—and realized I had made my first mistake, as he looked down his nose with a call-me-Mister-Chairman expression. I told him in a slow, easy, nonthreatening way that I would like to spend some time talking to him about S&L deregulation.

He just chopped me off: "Why don't you mind your own damn business?" he said and stomped out of the room.

St Germain was later described by author Brooks Jackson as "an extreme example of the way the political system encouraged waste, cheated the poor, and subsidized the rich, which in turn kept campaign funds and sometimes extra income flowing to the lawmakers who perpetuated the agreement." The S&L debacle went on to become the nation's worst financial scandal, one created entirely by the government in Washington.

Congress winked at the savings and loan scandal while it doled out billions in taxpayer dollars to pay for it—billions that could have created jobs and rebuilt cities. Congress subsidizes polluters who have the technology to produce environmentally friendly products but who refuse to because innovation is risky and might cut into profits. Under Ronald Reagan and George Bush, Congress funded—with bad checks—a gold-plated military that had less to do with maintaining military strength than it did with enriching ten or twelve big military contractors, despite their criminal records of fraud, price-fixing, and conspiracies to produce unsafe, shoddy products. All these things have contributed to our incredible debt, a shark of a debt that devours everything in its path and continues to grow because politicians must pay back the investments of those who finance their campaigns.

The huge rise in debt during the Reagan presidency was caused by a combination of factors including massive increases in military spending as well as reductions in taxes. This could not have happened without the participation of my fellow congressional Democrats. In addition to cutting taxes and raising military spending, Reagan, with the complicity of the Democratic-controlled Congress, gave huge tax breaks to the very same interest groups that were plying the politicians with campaign money. Government spending rose, but very little of that money "trickled down" to people who were not directly targeted for benefitting from the legislation.

There is no way to spend money unless Congress authorizes it. If Reagan's ideas were unsound, no one forced Congress, with its Democratic House majority, to go along. Good old Congress jacked up the deficits by increasing government spending, not only in terms of entitlements such as welfare and Medicaid but also in terms of payback to corporate benefactors. It was not just Democrats or just Republicans who were responsible for this reckless spending. Each party had a hand in it because each party was paying back its own private benefactors, its own special interests. In the 1980s, we saw deficit spending by two-party consensus creating a bipartisan debt. That is how the two major parties got us where we are today.

In some of their derelictions, congressional leaders say they were merely following the lead of a popular president. That is a lame excuse. Congress writes the legislation for government expenditures, but nowhere is it written that Congress is to be the rubber stamp of the president. The political battles of the last few years should be proof enough of that.

It is true that sometimes a forceful president—a Franklin Roosevelt or a Lyndon Johnson—will get his way. More often than not, though, the money trail leads to favors and expenditures made on behalf of large campaign contributors. All too often a bipartisan agreement really translates into a quid pro quo: I will vote for expenditures directed at your special interest if you will vote for expenditures directed at mine.

Perhaps we should make members of Congress sport logos and labels from their big campaign contributors. Then we could tell the senator representing big tobacco from the senator working for auto manufacturing. Behind this absurd image is an important question: If our elected officials speak for the special interests, who then will speak for the national interest and the American people?

In all legislative chambers, the way it works is this: the representatives of one big interest forever yield to the representatives of another big interest. He who pays the piper calls the tune. Since only 1/10 of 1 percent of Americans contribute more than $200 to any political candidate, the great majority of people are shut out of the political arena where special interests call the tunes.

Big donors give money to candidates running for office and are repaid tenfold, a hundredfold, even a thousandfold in government favors.

Here's one example: Between 1985 and 1990, the total contribution to the House and Senate from sugar interests exceeded $3.9 million. In 1985, both the House and Senate voted against reducing price supports and import restrictions after seventeen sugar PACs contributed more than $900,000 to congressional campaign coffers over a three-year period. The price supports, quotas, and import restrictions that the sugar industry received as the payback for its contributions added $3 billion annually to the cost American consumers pay for sugar. For an average of $780,000 per year in contributions, the extra $3 billion results in a return on investment (ROI) of 3,846:1.

The idea of "return on investment" is a new concept with regard to campaign finance. What it refers to is how much an interest group contributed to political candidates and parties and how much the interest group profited from legislation that the contribution bought. Were we to examine special interest legislation in terms of special interest campaign contributions, I am sure that we would find an ROI that is astronomical—sometimes 100:1, sometimes 1,000:1, sometimes more. Certainly, as we shall see, many special interests make more money investing in politicians than they do by investing in productive enterprise.

We do not have to have a government dominated by special interest money. It is constitutionally feasible, even under the awful *Buckley v. Valeo* ruling, to design a system of campaign finance that frees candidates from the need to take special interest money.

The point I want to make right now is that if we were to enact the Clean Money Campaign Reform system I described in chapter 2, members of Congress would not feel compelled to reward their big contributors with tax breaks and other legislative favors. In such a system, public funding would be available to those who eschew private funding of elections. It would cost taxpayers a small amount of money—approximately $6.50 per taxpayer per year. That $6.50 would generate a sizable return on investment *for taxpayers*. Freed from the need to raise millions of dollars from special interests, our elected officials could legislate on the basis of *public interest*, not campaign payback. Corporate welfare and other spending boondoggles could be controlled, if not eliminated. Spending could be cut—and the budget balanced—without destroying popular and necessary government programs.

Our system of taxation could be made simpler and more fair. As I will show in the next chapter, our hated tax system is not altogether the responsibility of an uncaring Internal Revenue Service. It is a product of political payola—the result of an unfair, undemocratic, money-driven campaign finance system.

Campaign Contributions and Unfair Taxes

The House Ways and Means Committee is supposed to deal with issues of government taxation, and as a member, I intended to be a voice for tax reform. My preference then was a simplified progressive tax code with a few targeted deductions that would encourage basic necessities like home ownership and college tuition. I also favored selected tax credits for environmentally sound, job-creating enterprise. Tax law is an essential tool for making public policy. My intent was, and is, to foster tax reform that advances the interests of the nation, not the special interests who make campaign contributions and expect something in return.

My ideas for tax reform seemed to me neither radical nor controversial. I thought that I would find a lot of support for a fair-minded tax code among my colleagues in Congress. Now, irrespective of what you think of it, the progressive—or graduated—income tax, with the rich paying a greater percentage of their income than the poor, dates back almost 100 years to the era of Teddy Roosevelt and Woodrow Wilson.

Over the years, however, members of Congress, as a way of paying back the individuals and interest groups that financed their campaigns, created so many loopholes that the progressive aspect of the tax code gradually eroded. The wealthy (individuals as well as corporations) with a cadre of smart tax lawyers, routinely exploited their ability to create loopholes in the tax code to avoid paying taxes. When no tax loophole existed, they got their beneficiaries in Congress to create one for them. Members of Congress, dependent as they are on campaign contributions, are in no position to resist doing their benefactors that kind of favor. In such instances, the benefactors wield a lot of power. If a member won't come through for them, they'll not only withhold their campaign contribution in the next election, but they might also give their contribution to that member's opponent.

Fairness—equality of opportunity and responsibility—is a prerequisite for a just society. If the tax code is designed to encourage social equality, no exception should be granted because someone gave the right person a campaign contribution. Because of this kind of special treatment applied through the tax code, most Americans are less than enthusiastic about contributing their "fair" share of taxes. The problem is, once you have an avenue by which to gain exception, you undermine the fairness of the entire system.

Can anyone really believe that there is not a simpler way to collect revenues for the management of our national finances? Perhaps it is a simplified progressive tax, a simple flat tax, or one with tiered rates. Regardless of the system, the nation needs a tax code that will be immune from the campaign contribution system and, at the same time, immune from manipulation. Is it necessary for our system of taxation to be so complicated that many of our citizens have to pay someone money to fill out their forms? Wouldn't it be simpler if taxes could be collected immediately at the point of a particular financial transaction—be it the sale of a car or the purchase of a house—instead of requiring people to fill out pages upon pages of forms to make sure they pay their fair share?

I am convinced that as long as we allow the campaign finance system as I've lived it to continue, we will abuse the public at large to the benefit of the few and our Treasury receipts will be affected adversely and unfairly. Campaign contributors will fight tooth and nail for the status quo because of their ability to influence the creation of loopholes.

Who benefits from maintaining the status quo? Maybe it's the members of the so-called "underground economy" who fork over little or no tax because they are paid largely in cash. Maybe it's the people who prepare tax returns and might suffer if the tax system were reformed to the point of making tax forms fit on a postcard. Those who certainly benefit are the campaign contributors who win custom-tailored loopholes by manipulating the people who write the tax laws: members of Congress.

When it comes to campaign fund-raising, members of the House Ways and Means Committee are in the proverbial catbird seat. A Ways and Means Committee assignment is among the most lucrative precisely because these members, along with those on the Senate Finance Committee, have jurisdiction over tax legislation. For example, in the 1996 elections, members who had served on the Ways and Means Committee in the 104th Congress received an average contribution of $910,299. Any time tax reform is on the legislative agenda, special interest lobbyists descend on Congress to make their pitch for favors.

Go through any tax bill and examine the fine print, all those little paragraphs and clauses where the tax favors are concealed. It's my contention that most of these provisions—the ones dealing with individual taxpayers and particular companies and industries—were bought with campaign contributions. How else do you explain a special provision that benefits just one single taxpayer or one specific company or business? Special interests give money and get tax favors in return. That's the way the system works under current campaign finance law. And it is the result of bribery—the only legalized system of bribery I know. These tax favors, totaling in aggregate many billions of dollars, break the budget. And, as they are financed by ordinary taxpayers, they are grossly unfair.

Simplifying the tax code and lowering everyone's income tax rates is always popular with the voters, but once tax reform gets into the hands of the tax code writers, campaign promises to curb spending take second place to the need to pay back campaign contributors. Special interest groups make contributions and hire pricey lobbyists (themselves big contributors) to make their case. And so it's not ordinary voters, but rather special-interest lobbyists, who have the decisive say in how tax bills are written.

Jimmy Carter ran for president attacking the tax code as "a disgrace to the human race" and a welfare program for the rich. I was drawn to his ideas for tax reform and as a member of Ways and Means looked forward to working with him on this issue. When he proposed to cut out some of the more egregious loopholes favoring the rich, my colleagues on the committee attacked his proposal and tore it to shreds.

One of the most unfair loopholes in the tax code—and a symbol for all that can go wrong with the code—was the "three martini lunch." While most working people brown-bag their lunch or grab a bite at a diner, a fast-food restaurant, a cafe, or a coffee shop, lawyers, businessmen, executives, accountants, bankers, and others are entitled, under the tax code, to wine and dine each other at expensive restaurants and, simply by talking business over their shrimp cocktails and martinis, deduct the cost of that meal from their taxes. The same exemption applies when those who buy luxury box seats at sporting events or front-row orchestra seats at concerts or the theater talk business. While most Americans pay the cost of their entertainment directly out of their earnings, those whom the tax code favors write their entertainment expenses off as a business tax deduction. Because those write-offs are lost to the government as revenue, in essence ordinary taxpayers not only pay for their own entertainment but, with their taxes, underwrite the entertainment of those who take advantage of this program.

There is absolutely no logical reason why working Americans have to subsidize this kind of exemption. The "three martini lunch" increases neither productivity nor business efficiency. (On the contrary, because people do not do their best work when stuffed and drunk, it probably lowers efficiency and productivity.) But the tax code allows it. President Carter failed in his effort to end the subsidy and the practice persists, though the deduction for most meal and entertainment expenses was reduced to 80 percent in 1986 and further lowered to 50 percent in the Revenue Reconciliation Act of 1993. It is one of the perks special interests get for financing American elections.

As Jeffrey H. Birnbaum and Alan S. Murray reported in their 1987 book about tax reform, *Showdown at Gucci Gulch*, President Carter's effort at reforming the tax code ended up as "a complete renunciation" of his fair-minded proposals. Instead of simplifying the tax code and giving a tax cut to low- and middle-income Americans, Congress loaded the bill with new tax benefits for special interests—particularly "farmers, teachers, Alaskan natives, railroads, record manufacturers, the Gallo winery of California, and two Arkansas chicken farmers."

The situation was summarized precisely in a 1983 book by Robert S. McIntyre and Dean C. Tipps, who are both with the non-profit, though admittedly liberal, watchdog organization called Citizens for Tax Justice. In *Inequity & Decline: How the Reagan Tax Policies Are Affecting the American Taxpayer and the Economy*, McIntyre and Tipps wrote, "In the 1978 revenue act . . . Congress did little for middle- and lower-income taxpayers while expanding corporate loopholes and reducing taxes on capital gains." By the time Carter left office, for every $1 it collected from corporations, the government collected $4 from individuals (*Inequity & Decline*, p. 13).

President Reagan campaigned in 1980 with promises of big tax cuts. As president, he did not disappoint his supporters. His 1981 tax bill, the Economic Recovery Tax Act, was designed to repay campaign contributors who financed the 1980 election and to attract more contributions for the 1982 congressional elections. With the support of the Democratic majority in Congress, which, thanks to Tony Coelho, was also focused on raising money for the next election, the bill passed. I voted for it, thinking it was better than what we had.

The 1981 tax bill included numerous amendments custom-crafted to suit both parties' big campaign contributors. It seemed to me that my colleagues in Congress were engaged in a special interest bidding war. Democrats competed with Republicans to prove themselves more generous to the special interest groups in supporting tax giveaways. As a member of Ways and Means, I was engaged in fighting these giveaways in committee hearings. But the most important activity was apparently taking place behind the scenes. McIntyre and Tipps quote then-Senator Paul Laxalt (R-NV) (who now operates his own lobbying firm, The Laxalt Group) as crowing, "One of the greatest things that was done was to go through the lists of big contributors and get them to lean on swing people. If a big contributor calls and says, 'Go along with this,' it has an effect."

A tax bill is long and complex. Many of the concepts are arcane and are written in a style that no one except lobbyists, lawyers, and those who draft the bill understand. Giveaways are tucked in the fine print. Very few legislators who vote for the bill are likely to know exactly who will get the money they give away so cavalierly. Moreover, it is only in the last few years that computer technology has been widely available, allowing watchdog groups and journalists to analyze, industry by industry, federal election campaign data.

We do not now, and probably never will, have an accurate tally of how much money passed to federal candidates from labor unions, environmental groups, and oil, gas, electric utility, telephone, chemical, and other big corporations to federal candidates during the 1970s and early 1980s. By examining what special interests gave to candidates in recent years, we can estimate what they gave before disclosure was required and public records were kept. In many cases, the aggregate contributions from a specific industry equal tens of millions of dollars. That is a lot of money to be giving political candidates and their parties, but it is "small potatoes" compared to the rate of return on the investment.

The fact is that for the millions of dollars that special interests were giving, they were reaping billions in tax favors—billions that came out of taxpayers' wallets. This giveaway that started in the 1970s and 1980s continues unabated today. In a sense, elected officials serve as middlemen who transform campaign contributions into corporate profits.

Just to be clear, I don't care if it's a business or consumer group doing the giving. It's just plain wrong if the intention is to gain special influence or access. The simple fact is that business interests outspend others by seven to one.

One of the biggest boondoggles on the 1981 tax bill involved the accelerated cost recovery system (ACRS), euphemistically known as depreciation reform. ACRS allowed corporations to depreciate investments much faster than the previous tax law had allowed. Birnbaum and Murray, in *Showdown at Gucci Gulch*, rightly pegged ACRS as an enormous boon to corporate America. "It was an extraordinarily rich tax worth hundreds of billions of dollars to business," they wrote.

Depreciation reform first reared its head in 1978, but opponents of it, like myself, were successful in keeping it out of that year's tax bill. Corporate America wanted this tax break very much and had invested in Congress heavily. After the 1978 tax bill passed, business lobbyists continued to push depreciation reform.

As the 1981 tax bill took shape in Congress, other members and I began to express concern about the size of the giveaways. I, like other opponents, thought that the president was giving too much money away to the private sector and that, because of these giveaways, the budget deficit was going to cause problems for the economy down the road. Treasury Secretary Don Regan responded to our criticisms by declaring the administration's intention to scale back the ACRS program. This response led to what Washington insiders called a "Lear Jet Weekend."

"Over the weekend of June 7 and 8, the sky over the Capitol was dark with Lear Jets, as America's leading corporate executives descended on Washington intent on restoring ACRS to its original dimensions," McIntyre and Tipps wrote. The pressure of so many heavy-hitting campaign contributors lobbying for ACRS worked. On Monday, June 9, the Reagan administration announced that it was not only restoring the ACRS to its former dimensions but actually adding new provisions that would make it even more extravagant. One of the additions to the administration bill was a provision allowing companies to buy and sell tax breaks.

Tax leasing was a tax boon for those corporations that, by virtue of other tax write-offs, did not owe any corporate taxes. Under the provisions of tax leasing, these corporations were allowed to sell their excess tax credits and deductions to other firms by entering into arrangements that came to be known as "safe-harbor leasing."

Safe-harbor leasing is typical of how the tax code is conceptualized. No one but the lobbyists pushing it and the members of Congress drafting it fully understood what the provision was all about. Certainly the public had no understanding that safe-harbor leases represented a massive tax break for corporations. Consequently, there was no protest. Taxpayers did not know they were getting fleeced. In all, about 80 percent of the tax savings from depreciation reform went to the country's largest 2,000 firms—the top .1 percent of America's businesses. The cost, of course, was absorbed by the U.S. Treasury. So, while President Reagan was denouncing Cadillac-driving welfare queens, big business was picking billions from taxpayer pockets.

In *Inequity & Decline* (p. 33), McIntyre and Tipps provide a breakdown of the money ACRS funnelled to corporate America during the 1980s:

- Tax breaks for oil and gas tax interests, at least $60 billion
- Reductions in the oil windfall profits tax, $20 to $30 billion
- Tax breaks for mining companies, $10 billion
- Tax breaks for the chemical industry, approximately $15 billion
- Tax breaks for electric and natural gas utilities, $30 billion
- Tax breaks for telephone companies, $40 billion
- Tax breaks for railroads, approximately $8 billion
- Total giveaway to large corporations from the American taxpayer, $260 billion

The 1981 tax bill caused the nation's debt to explode from $909 billion in the last year of Carter's presidency to $1.56 trillion after

Ronald Reagan's first term in office. A tax bill passed in 1982 somewhat remedied the excesses of the previous year's giveaway, but the damage had been done. We are still paying for it.

The Deficit Reduction Act of 1984, more than 800 pages long, was ostensibly drafted to ease the transition between old and new tax laws. Transition rules, designed to help companies adjust to the new tax laws, represented the "meat" of the bill. In actuality, however, transition rules were just another way to dispense legislative favors to campaign contributors. The chairmen of the two congressional tax-writing committees doled out tax giveaways to individual members as a way of gaining their support for final legislation.

You don't read about transition rules in the daily newspaper. As giveaways they are hidden away in the fine print of tax legislation. To find out about them you have to study specialty publications like Washington D.C.'s *National Journal.* Transition rules gave tax benefits worth billions of dollars to certain companies in certain members' state or congressional districts. The transition rules in the 1984 bill, according to a *National Journal* article titled "Lawyers Reap a Bonanza from the 1984 Tax Law; Billions in Special Loopholes" (13 August 1984), ranged from special provisions for Amex Inc., Levi Strauss & Co., and Warner-Amex to estate-tax relief for wealthy families like the Halls, who own Hallmark Cards, and the Hunts, a family of Texas oilmen, and a thicket of special rules for insurance companies.

Transition rules, by their nature, have nothing to do with public interest or national priorities. They should be seen for what they are: political payola, the return on investment that corporations get for their campaign contributions.

The proof is in the way the rules are worded. The aforementioned article in the *National Journal* described one special rule as written specifically for an unnamed insurance company whose "accrual of discount less amortization of premium for bonds and short-term investments (as shown in the first footnote to Exhibit 3 of its 1983 annual statements) . . . exceeds $72,000,000 but does not exceed $73,000,000." Only one company, Massachusetts Mutual Life Insurance, fit that description.

You can bet that the member of Congress who sponsored that rule did not do so because he knew that the financial success of that one insurance company was important to the public interest. Here's a much more likely scenario: that obscure and very specific clause was drafted by insurance company lawyers and inserted in the tax bill at the behest of company lobbyists and agreed upon by members of Congress as a way of saying "thank you" for past campaign contributions. And the Massachusetts Mutual Life Insurance Company was not alone in fleecing the American taxpayer. Insurance companies in Alabama, Oklahoma, Texas, and Arkansas and the Capital Holding Company of Louisville, Kentucky, benefitted from similar custom-crafted provisions.

Another provision in the law benefitted some of the nation's largest corporations, including Citibank, IBM, Exxon, and GTE. These companies, on the basis of the opinions of their own tax lawyers, had set up financing subsidiaries in the Netherlands Antilles, a part of the West Indies. According to the lawyers' opinions, these subsidiaries were entitled to take advantage of lower European interest rates without paying the 30 percent withholding tax that the Internal Revenue Service normally imposes on interest payments sent abroad. Unfortunately for the companies, the IRS rejected this interpretation and demanded that the companies pay the withholding tax. During a meeting of the conference committee drafting the 1984 Deficit Reduction Act, Representative Barber Conable (R-NY), the retiring minority leader of the House Ways and Means Committee, inserted a change in the law that retroactively validated the tax lawyers' opinions. In other words, the law was drafted to reverse the decision of the IRS and negate the 30 percent withholding payments.

In 1985, during my last term in Congress, Representative Dick Gephardt (D-MO) and Senator Bill Bradley (D-NJ) teamed up and pushed for a simplified tax code that would close loopholes and create three slightly progressive tax rates (14 percent, 16 percent, and 30 percent). President Reagan backed these ideas, as did Chairman of the House Ways and Means Committee Dan Rostenkowski. As recalled by Birnbaum and Murray in *Showdown at Gucci Gulch* (p. 99), Rostenkowski, speaking for the Democratic party, told a television audience,

> Even if you can't spell Rostenkowski, put down what they used to call my father and grandfather—Rosty. . . . Just address it to R-O-S-T-Y, Washington, D.C. The post office will get it to me. Better yet, write your representative and your senator. And stand up for fairness and lower taxes.

More than 75,000 people wrote to "Rosty, Washington, D.C." One person even sent him a two-by-four board so he could beat back special interests.

Special interests had little use for planks of wood to beat back the taxpayers. They had already greased the legislative course with campaign money. As the tax reform bill went into mark-up,[1] the special interests were poised to reap the rewards of their political investments. According to Birnbaum and Murray (p. 180), in 1985 congressional tax writers received $19.8 million in campaign contributions.

Considering it was not even an election year, that was a remarkably large sum. Special interest PACs donated $6.7 million of the total. The twenty members of the Senate Finance Committee banked a total of $11.8 million in 1985, up from $6.4 million in 1983. The thirty-six members of the Ways and Means Committee received nearly $8 million in 1985, up from $3.5 million two years earlier. Actually, that was thirty-five members on the House Ways and Means Committee because I, as always, planned to run for re-election with my own money. I didn't need, nor did I accept, contributions.

Among the top Ways and Means fund-raisers were Sam Gibbons (D-FL), who took in $317,096; Henson Moore (R-LA), who got $333,620; and James Jones (D-OK), who received $343,592.

---

1. Mark-up is the process that occurs when proposed legislation goes to committee and is discussed, amended, and otherwise dealt with by the members of the committee and during which a significant amount of influence can be brought to bear by special interests.

Dan Rostenkowski, no slouch himself when it came to raising money for a House seat that was never seriously contested, pronounced himself nauseated by the fund-raising orgy.

Ronnie G. Flippo (D-AL) typified the relationship between Ways and Means Committee members and campaign fund-raising. A long-term member of Ways and Means who rarely faced opposition in his rural Alabama district, Flippo raised $287,000 from PACs during the 1985-1986 election cycle. Among his corporate benefactors were five New York banks, the American Bankers Association— which gave him $20,000—the Chicago Board of Trade and Mercantile Exchange, two sugar beet associations, the American Medical Association, the American Dental Association, and dozens of other interest groups all affected by tax reform. The late Phil Stern founded the National Library for Money and Politics and compiled this data; Stern pointed out that none of those interest groups had much of a constituency in rural Alabama.

Representative Wyche Fowler (D-GA) was another member of the House Ways and Means Committee who excelled at raising money. Planning to run for Senate in 1986, he notified the congressional tax staff that he intended to fight for a long list of special tax breaks. In 1985, Fowler received $539,575 in campaign contributions from a host of special interest groups and wealthy donors with keen interests in the tax bill, including a New York tax-shelter promoter as well as Texas oil drillers and real estate developers. The connections are transparent. The tax breaks Fowler was fighting for were essentially payoffs for campaign contributions. I'm not accusing Fowler, Flippo, and my other colleagues on the Ways and Means Committee of doing anything illegal. What is most disgusting about these campaign contributions and the favors they bought is that they were *all* legal.

Members of Ways and Means as well as Senate Finance Committee members easily sabotaged the 1986 reform bill by stuffing it with more than 400 transition rules. Critics called the bill the "Lobbyists Full Employment Act." When the Ways and Means

Committee first started considering the bill, I observed that certain members seemed to be serving as champions for specific special interests. These committee members and their staffs worked hand-in-hand with favored lobbyists, alerting lobbyists on what parts of the bill were important to their clients and consulting together on the proper wording of each special interest clause.

A personal word on Flippo and Fowler: I considered both of them to be highly ethical legislators. When they decided to seek higher office—Flippo as governor of Alabama and Fowler as senator from Georgia—they found it necessary to compromise their principles as they sought funds to pursue those posts.

The Tax Reform Act of 1986 created additional loopholes—$5 billion worth, according to Birnbaum and Murray. The word loophole, when used by politicians, is a distortion of its actual meaning. Loophole suggests a politician's innocence, as if tax breaks were written into laws by mistake. Loophole implies that sharp-eyed lawyers and accountants exploit legislators' good intentions and then use the well-meaning laws in sly and tricky ways. That is not the case. A loophole is a deliberate legislative ploy that creates a legal way for politicians to pay back financial benefactors.

I recall the weeks leading up to the vote on the 1986 tax reform bill as a fund-raising orgy. Lobbyists descended on the House proffering gifts and offering money to members. All the lobbyists wanted was members' support for obscure clauses and passages in the legislation that would favor the particular industry or special interest they represented. The members were glad to have a chance to raise money for the next election. Jeffrey Birnbaum and Alan S. Murray, in *Showdown at Gucci Gulch,* described the frenzy just as I remember it.

> Washington was a virtual money machine, and lobbyists provided much of the fuel. Fund-raisers of one kind or another were held almost every night of the week, and lobbyists would stuff checks in [politicians'] pockets and jump from one to another. It was as if there were a nightly sale,

and the members of Congress were the merchandise. Evenings were filled with so much drinking and eating at fund-raiser cocktail parties that several of the lobbyists in town had to put themselves on controlled fasts under the care of a diet doctor during the tax-reform effort.

I need to be clear about what I mean when I talk about corporations. An odd thing about American capitalism is that small firms, which are the source of most new jobs and most new technological innovation, tend to play by the rules. They are too busy struggling to survive to hire expensive lobbyists and ply politicians with huge campaign contributions. The true culprits are the politicians who give a great return on investment to the special interests—the multinationals and the conglomerates, among others—who bribe politicians writing tax laws and then benefit from the tax favors written into law in exchange for the bribes. This rips off the American taxpayer. It also gives corporate giants a competitive advantage over smaller competitors that cannot afford big contributions and hence must pay the taxes that their big competitors successfully avoid.

Giant corporations, however, are not the only ones paying very low tax rates. The 1986 bill failed to address the problem of very rich individuals who use loopholes to avoid paying income taxes altogether. Contrary to the fairness that Reagan promised the American people, the 1986 bill shifted the tax burden from corporations to the middle class.

In the 1950s, when America was the economic powerhouse of the world, corporations paid a much higher tax rate than they do today. In 1954, for example, corporations paid 75¢ in taxes for every $1.00 paid by individuals and families. As a result of the 1986 reform, the ratio between corporate and individual rates changed in favor of the corporations. By 1994, corporations were paying about 20¢ for every $1.00 paid by individuals and families.

When the share of corporate taxes falls, tax revenues have to be made up by individuals and families. If corporations today paid taxes at the same rates they paid during the 1950s, federal tax revenues would rise by about $250 billion a year. That is roughly two and one-half times the amount corporations currently pay. That $250 billion would wipe out the current budget deficit and leave an enormous surplus. In their book, *America: Who Really Pays the Taxes?* (p. 140), Philadelphia *Inquirer* reporters Donald L. Barlett and James B. Steele point out that these loopholes cost American taxpayers $5 billion. That is enough money to provide a 60 percent tax cut for everyone with an income below $200,000.

Promoted as a law that would bring fairness back to the tax system and eliminate loopholes, the 1986 tax reform represented yet another legal raid on the U.S. Treasury by the special interests from which political candidates get most of their money. Although the bill was sold to the public as tax relief for the middle class, the rich benefitted most. As Barlett and Steele wrote, "[I]n 1985, the year before the tax overhaul bill was passed, those with incomes between $30,000 and $40,000 paid combined federal income and Social Security taxes of $6,663. That was 19 percent of their income. In 1989, three years after tax reform, they paid $6,177, or 17.6 percent. That amounted to a 7 percent cut in tax rates."

"By comparison," Barlett and Steele continued, "during the same period, those with incomes between $500,000 and $1 million saw their combined taxes fall from $243,506 to $168,714. That amounted to a 31 percent cut in tax rates—nearly five times the rate-cut for middle-class taxpayers." Moreover, the average tax bill of a millionaire fell 27 percent, dropping from $864,068 to $634,196—a tax savings of $229,873.

"A comparison with individuals and families who reported incomes of more than $1 million in 1980 is even more stark. From 1980 to 1989, their average tax bill . . . plunged from $980,869 to $634,196. That amounted to a 35 percent tax cut, giving those people $246,673 extra in spending money."

The Clinton tax reform of 1993, with its earned income credit, gave some tax relief to the working poor but did not crack down on millionaire scofflaws. Although the top tax rate rose from 31 percent to 39.6 percent for families earning more than $250,000, nothing was done to close existing loopholes. The result is that multimillionaires continue to use the tax code to avoid paying taxes—legally.

In April 1997, *The New York Times* reported that the latest available information from the Internal Revenue Service showed nearly 2,400 of the Americans with the highest incomes paid no federal income taxes in 1993, up from 85 individuals and couples in 1977 (*New York Times*, 18 April 1997, A1). Another 18,000 individuals with high incomes paid less than 5 percent of their income in taxes. Experts cite the inadequacies of the 1986 tax reform as well as cutbacks in IRS auditing as reasons for the increase in tax avoidance. As the *Times* put it, ". . . in the past decade the agency had significantly reduced its audits of people with the highest incomes while increasing audits of those with the lowest."

It is common for members of Congress to berate the IRS, but to my knowledge no one in Congress has ever accused the tax enforcers of letting wealthy taxpayers off easy. The trickle-down argument for regressive tax codes suggests that corporations will invest their profits in well-paying jobs that will help America prosper. However, economic data do not bear this out.

Citizens for Tax Justice studied the tax subsidies and payments of the ten largest corporations that engaged in large-scale layoffs during the period from 1992 to 1995.[2] Together, these companies laid off 134,450 workers in their American operations while paying their CEOs, in 1995, an average of $5.2 million each. The ten companies combined had pretax profits of $60.7 billion during the three-year period and, in addition, successfully got a total of $8.3 billion in tax subsidies—paid for by the working Americans who actually do pay taxes. Together, these ten corporations paid an average tax rate of 21.3 percent, lower than the 28 percent that most middle-income people have to pay the IRS.

---

2. The companies include AT&T, Kimberly-Clark, BankAmerica, Eastman Kodak, Amoco, Procter & Gamble, American Home Products, Mobil, Allied Signal, and MCI.

Because of the propensity of Congress to grant special favors to special interests, the argument can easily be made that a visible result has been to shift even more wealth to those who already have most of it. During the 1950s, the richest 1 percent owned between 30 percent to 35 percent of the wealth in America. During the Carter administration, their share dropped to less than 25 percent for the first time in the last half-century. Then, thanks to Reaganomics and the complicity of many Democrats in Congress, the amount of wealth owned by the richest 1 percent of families in America rose to more than 40 percent of the wealth owned by the nation.

Why can't Congress come up with a simple tax code that treats all people fairly? It does not take great imagination to outline such reform. Such a system—simple, obvious, and as American as apple pie—does not have a chance in the current political climate because of the influence that campaign contributions wield over the political process. No candidate wants to be accused of raising taxes no matter whose they are. Candidates—Republican and Democrat alike—are desperate in their need for money to run for and win political office. And most big contributors are not likely to give money to those who want to raise taxes.

According to one study of campaign giving, less than 1/10 of 1 percent of the voting public gives 77 percent of the campaign money raised by candidates for Congress. As long as candidates are dependent upon that small fraction of the population, a fair and equitable tax system is not going to get far on the congressional agenda.

For reform to happen, we must insulate members of Congress from the influence of special interests. There is only one constitutional way to do this, and that is by instituting the Clean Money Campaign Reform. Under this reform, congressional candidates who agree not to raise private money would have the opportunity to run clean campaigns with Clean Money—public funds. If such a system were enacted, the chairs and committee members of the House Ways and Means Committee and the Senate Finance Committee would no longer be under pressure to give tax breaks as payoffs for campaign contributions.

CHAPTER SEVEN

Defense Policy
for Sale

A s a World War II veteran whose congressional district included Pearl Harbor, I certainly know the importance of a strong military defense. Over the years, trillions of taxpayer dollars have gone to the Pentagon, but not all that money has been strictly related to keeping our nation strong.

The willingness of Americans to support military spending is linked to issues other than simple national defense. Many people see supporting a strong military as a patriotic duty, a source of pride. Others, though they do not always openly admit it, see supporting the military as akin to supporting a jobs program. Some politicians, for example, who oppose publicly funded programs for job creation are more than happy to support military spending programs—especially if those programs provide jobs for people in their states and districts. Other politicians use the military budget as, in part, a payoff to the defense industry, which gives politicians millions of dollars in campaign contributions and expects a generous return on its investment.

The late Charles E. Wilson went from being head of General Motors (GM) to being President Dwight D. Eisenhower's secretary of defense. Known as "Engine Charlie," Wilson has long symbolized the conflict of interest inherent in the Pentagon's inflated budget. During the Second World War, when Wilson was chairman of General Motors, he helped convert GM's automobile assembly lines into full-scale military arms production lines. When he became the head of the Pentagon, Wilson worked hard and successfully to maintain a high level of military spending, but his goal was not merely to keep our nation strong. He also wanted to ensure that GM would be in a position to reap huge military contracts on a profitable "cost-plus" basis, in addition to making money from car and truck sales.

During his confirmation hearings, Democratic senators demanded that Wilson sell $7 million worth of personal stock, including $2.5 million worth of GM holdings. In a famous remark that summed up the symbiotic relationship between government and the defense industry, Wilson argued that his corporate holdings did not represent a conflict of interest. "What is good for our country," he said, "is good for General Motors and vice versa."

Certainly, Wilson's statement had the ring of truth. When GM has prospered, the country has prospered. Men and women working for GM make good money, which helps the economy and should, in turn, increase tax revenues. GM's primary commitment, of course, is neither to its workers nor to the nation. Like all private businesses, its commitment is to making a profit for its owners, the shareholders. As is the case with other corporations, GM has always been willing to invest in politicians to secure government support for its economic activities.

In the 1994 election cycle, the defense industry contributed $8.6 million to members of Congress. Most of that money went to members sitting on defense-related committees. This sum is approximately the same amount the defense industry gave to candidates over the entire ten-year span I was in Congress. General Motors alone, through its PACs and executives, gave contributions totalling $215,984 to members of defense-related committees in 1994. Lockheed and Martin Marietta (which merged in 1995 and became Lockheed Martin) together gave $1.1 million, and ten other defense contractors gave even more money than General Motors. Of this money, $1.7 million was distributed to members of the House Armed Services Committee. General Dynamics, McDonnell Douglas, and Loral distributed more than $100,000 each.

I want to point out an interesting anomaly in this pattern of campaign giving. I discovered it by using data developed by the Center for Responsive Politics (CRP), a nonprofit, nonpartisan research group that developed new methods and models for using computers to analyze campaign finance data. As CRP research shows, the chairs of most congressional committees get huge contributions from the industries and corporations they oversee. Representative Ron Dellums (D-CA), however, who rose to chair the House Armed Services Committee because of seniority, received only $20,900 from the defense industry, while fourteen rank-and-file members received more than $50,000 each.

In one sense, it is understandable that the defense industry would give more money to the rank-and-file committee members than they would to Dellums. Throughout his long tenure in Congress, Dellums, who opposed the Vietnam War and favors cutting the military budget, has been an outspoken dove. The other members of the Armed Forces Committee were more sympathetic to the Pentagon's agenda, and the industry had reason to want them to have the campaign resources to remain in power.

The then-ranking Republican of the House Armed Forces Committee, Floyd Spence (SC), received $60,000 from military contributors for the 1994 election. That chunk represented a full third of the total amount he received from all contributors. Spence, first elected in 1970, was a veteran legislator by the 1990s and hardly needed the money; he wound up the 1994 election with $82,000 (out of a total $179,000) still in the bank. Nevertheless, as majority leader on the House committee beginning with the 1995 session, Spence began collecting even more military money—$115,800 for the 1996 election.

73

Members of Congress who favor an industry's given position are rewarded with campaign contributions. Consequently, pro-industry politicians have a decided financial advantage during an election campaign. With regard to defense issues, the prospect of contributions from the defense industry encourages politicians to temper their criticisms of military spending.

It's true that candidates do not necessarily need money from the defense industry. Dellums, for example, gets a large proportion of his campaign contributions from labor unions and is very popular in his left-of-center East Bay Area district. He does not need military money that badly, but candidates in tight races need all the money they can get. The defense industry gives supportive politicians hundreds of thousands of dollars. That money goes a long way. It buys lots of advertising and finances plenty of other campaign necessities—not to mention the advantage it gives supporters over dovish opponents who do not get defense industry money.

While it's understandable the supporters of military spending would get more contributions from the defense industry than its opponents, it's not fair and it's undemocratic. Hawks and doves should run with equal resources. The public should be able to vote for the candidates it wants without the contest being distorted by the contributions of those with a financial vested interest in the outcome.

The defense-related issues members of Congress debate rarely reach the magnitude of war and peace. More frequently, defense-related congressional committees deal with issues of military procurement, a process that provides a truly remarkable example of government waste and inefficiency. Much of the preliminary work regarding military procurement is conducted by over 800 advisory boards—the major communications conduit linking the industry and the Pentagon. Made up of experts, these committees discuss military needs and industry capabilities. They do this out of public earshot, too, since the information they share often involves secret weapon systems and issues of national security. Unfortunately, these advisory committees are also self-selecting. Members come from within the defense community and dissident viewpoints are rarely represented, which means the public is not always well served by the committees' private conversations.

That the federal government's military procurement needs are discussed and reviewed by members of the defense community creates such a cozy relationship between the public (meaning the Pentagon) and private sectors that conflicts of interest cannot be avoided. Congressional oversight does not enter into the picture until after Pentagon needs have been discussed with industry representatives and often with sympathetic members of Congress. By the time Congress votes on the defense budget, most of the discussions about military priorities have already taken place. Most of the contractual agreements have been discussed, if not sealed as well.

Members of Congress who wish to seriously question what the Pentagon and its industry allies want are in a tough position. They risk being denounced as antimilitary and unpatriotic, whether such labels are true or not. On a more practical level, military spending critics such as Representative Dellums sacrifice their access to campaign contributions.

As I was leaving Congress, journalist Richard Stubbing published an excellent book titled *The Defense Game: An Insider Explores the Astonishing Realities of America's Defense Establishment* (Harper & Row, 1986), which provided an accurate description of "the rules of engagement," the process by which Congress and the Pentagon come to an agreement on the military budget. One of the first rules Stubbing described was that the Pentagon should include "cut insurance" in its initial spending request. Cut insurance refers to the Pentagon practice of asking for more than the military spenders either want or need. This gives members of Congress the opportunity to seem responsible by trimming the fat from a bloated budget. Because the budget has been bloated deliberately, everyone comes out a winner: the Pentagon and the defense contractors do not want that which is cut, and members of Congress can pretend they have exercised fiscal responsibility.

Cut insurance, of course, is hardly necessary in the current Congress where Republican hawks, for ideological and financial reasons, want to spend more money on the military than the Pentagon even requests. But as a way of doing business, it inflates the budget and is another example of an industry subsidy that comes at the taxpayers' expense.

Another one of Stubbing's rules of engagement was that members should "make noise, not action, on major defense issues." As Stubbing explained, "Members of Congress feel perfectly at ease conducting widely publicized hearings or making inflammatory statements which criticize Pentagon programs, policies, and managerial practices. They hesitate, however, to make specific cuts or changes which are not viewed as acceptable by leaders in the Pentagon. . . . While Congress is often a sounding board for Pentagon criticisms, it is almost never the place where important reforms or programs are enacted."

A third rule was, naturally, to add pork. The saying that pork greases the legislative wheels is as true when it comes to defense spending as it is with any other area of government spending. Stubbing said it very well when he observed, "Though the defense spending total is reduced each year as part of the cut-insurance game, the congressional defense budget typically includes several billion dollars in add-ons not requested by the Pentagon. . . . The vast majority of these add-ons are motivated primarily by pork-barrel interests." By agreeing to spend money and provide jobs in the states and congressional districts of key members of Congress, the Pentagon buys members' support for the entire military budget.

My experience in Congress was true to Stubbing's book. As a congressman during Reagan's presidency, I watched PAC contributions from the defense industry triple—specifically between 1980 and 1986. Though only 18 percent of the members in both houses of Congress sit on committees dealing with defense issues, the ten top defense contractors gave those members 47 percent of their gifts. As

I indicated earlier, ranking committee members tended to get more money than other members.

In the House, the two main committees that address military issues are the Armed Services Committee, which makes decisions on weapon systems and military budget priorities, and the Appropriations Committee, which allocates the money. As Phil Stern pointed out, Representative Bill Chappell (D-FL), who headed the House Defense Appropriations subcommittee, received more than $343,000 from defense industry PACs during the period 1979-1986. Representative William Dickinson (R-AL), who was the ranking Republican on the House Armed Services Committee during the early Reagan years, received more than $268,000. Even though both congressmen were hawks receiving a great deal of money from the defense industry, neither voted necessarily to please that industry. Instead of getting votes for their contributions to these men, the defense industry simply helped secure their incumbency—two hawks in Congress are better than two doves. Few challengers ever had the ability to match the amount of money military contractors gave to their congressional allies.

Little has changed in the ensuing years. A Democrat now sits in the White House and Republicans control the Congress. Nonetheless, defense industry money flows to those members of Congress who have decision-making power over military matters.

When I was in Congress, it was difficult to accurately track campaign contributions, but today, computer technology allows groups such as the Center for Responsive Politics to accurately report who gets and gives campaign money. In 1996, the CRP studied the relationship between campaign contributions and congressional voting patterns on military-related issues in the 104th Congress—specifically, spending on (1) the B-2 bomber, (2) the Arms Export Control Act, and (3) the F-22 fighter jets. The pattern of contributions was far from surprising: members of Congress who supported military spending received more money from defense contractors than their less spendthrift opponents.

What follows is a summation of the information the CRP culled regarding each of three issues. First, during the Reagan years, Congress allotted $44 billion for the construction of twenty B-2 bombers. Despite the end of the Cold War and the Air Force's insistence that it did not need any more of these high-tech planes, Northrop Grumman pushed the program heavily. In September 1995, the House voted 213 to 210 to continue the program. The 213 B-2 supporters each received an average of $2,073 from Northrop Grumman. Opponents of the bomber received on average $113. In 1996, when appropriations for the B-2 program were to be voted on in Congress, Northrop Grumman's PAC gave members more than $600,000 in campaign contributions as well as tours of its plant. No longer able to promote the bomber as a Cold War necessity, contractors said the appropriations would serve as a job-protection program.

Second, with regard to the Arms Export Control Act, the end of the Cold War and the furor over the budget deficit represented a crisis for America's arms manufacturers. If the United States was going to cut back on military spending, the defense industry would have to seek other markets for its wares.

Do the world's countries really need more arms? Are we troubled if certain foreign countries, when the United States sells them arms, sometimes use those arms against their own people, against our allies, and sometimes against us? Answer as you like, but recognize that these are matters needing open debate. CRP found that PACs representing defense exporters greased the passage of the Arms Export bill with contributions to members of Congress totalling more than $5.8 million. In the House, where the bill passed 276 to 152, supporters of arms exports each received an average of $12,454 from related PACs. Opponents got $4,785.

Finally, though American F-15 fighter jets dominated the skies, the Air Force wanted a more modern fighter—it wanted the F-22. In 1995, Congress appropriated $2 billion to begin construction of the F-22 fighter jet. Even in cases when it's clear the military wants a weapons system, money is evident. According to CRP research, the primary contractor, Lockheed Martin, helped the jet's cause by distributing more than $1.3 million in PAC contributions and soft money. Major subcontractors added another $1.2 million.

The defense industry knows no bounds in its quest for government money for a return on investment. If it cannot convince Congress that a military program is vital to national security, it falls back, as we have seen, on the "job creation" gambit. This is where the industry's hypocrisy is extraordinarily blatant, even for politics. On the one hand, defense contractors present themselves as vital cogs in the domestic economy, and so they are. Defense work is often unionized and well paying; working in a defense plant is one of the better blue-collar jobs. In pursuit of pleasing their stockholders, though, defense contractors never shy away from laying off workers. Indeed, thousands of workers have been laid off in the recent rash of corporate mergers.

In a particularly brazen mugging of the American taxpayer, certain defense corporations in the process of merging "persuaded" Congress to reimburse them for the costs of consolidation. The corporations included Grumman, Northrop, Lockheed, Martin Marietta, Boeing, and McDonnell Douglas (by the way, McDonnell Douglas used to be two separate companies). Congress gave these defense contractors more than $160 million in government subsidies, ostensibly to help them cover the costs of their mergers, but I believe it was actually to thank them for generous contributions totalling $10,655,806. The contributions went to both Republican and Democratic candidates and parties in the 1996 election cycle. That 15:1 rate of return does not include the $855 million Lockheed Martin requested as a subsidy to cover the costs of its corporate integration.

Giving defense corporations money to merge so that shareholders, corporate lawyers, and investment bankers can make a financial killing is not a reasonable way to protect our country. Our military budget should be based on the need for security and that alone. I am not going to say that the defense industry does not, at times, need some form of government help. The defense industry plays a vital role in protecting our country, and there may legitimately be times the industry should receive government assistance in the form of taxpayer subsidies. As I see it, subsidization is not the issue. The issue is how our country's leaders go about determining military priorities. This is where the campaign finance system impinges on rational discussion and merit-based decision making.

Under Clean Money Campaign Reform, defense contractors would still be able to lend their expertise in lobbying efforts. They could also tell members of Congress which programs they want to build and why they think we need them. That is free speech and their First Amendment right. But Congress should then make its decision on the basis of national interest. The campaign contributions that the defense industry gives to Congress undermine rational debate and make an objective decision impossible.

Under the current system, there is no congressional oversight of the Pentagon and its military contractors. Price-fixing, overcharging, and shoddy workmanship have become all too common. If caught, military contractors get their hands slapped. They can then go back to Congress for more contracts. Because there is no incentive for the defense industry to work efficiently and cut costs, the cycle of lawlessness repeats itself.

The following list was compiled by The Project on Government Oversight (POGO), a nonpartisan, nonprofit government watchdog agency whose mission is to "investigate and expose abuse of power, mismanagement, and acquiescence to corporate interests by the federal government." In 1995 and 1997, POGO published its review of legal actions taken by the federal government (dating back to the late 1980s) against the leading defense contractors. The results looked like this:

1. Lockheed Martin
   (a) Lockheed
      - $6.3 million to settle allegations that the company withheld cost information that inflated the contract price

- $500,000 to settle allegations that Randtron Systems Incorporated, a unit of Lockheed, did not give the government relevant information that would have lowered the price of military contracts for radar antennas

(b) Lockheed Martin Corporation

- $5.3 million to settle allegations that the company deliberately bid low to win a contract then made up the shortfall by boosting research and development costs

2. McDonnell Douglas
   - Defective Pricing, $1.38 million settlement
   - Defective Pricing, $1 million settlement
   - Defective Pricing, $7.5 million settlement
   - Defective Pricing, $12.2 million settlement

3. General Motors (Hughes Electronics Corporation)

(a) Hughes

- Paid $4.05 million to settle a suit alleging that the company failed to perform tests on electronic equipment for the military
- False Statement, $3.5 million criminal fine
- Mischarging, $275,000 settlement
- Product Substitution, found guilty and received a $500,000 fine
- Defective Pricing, $11 million
- Obstruction of Justice, vice president received ten years in prison and a $250,000 fine
- Kickbacks, engineer fined $5,000 and received three years probation
- Conspiracy/Conversion of Classified Documents, $3.6 million and civil settlements, $50,000 reimbursement of investigation, $50,000 removal of overhead claims

- Procurement Fraud, pled guilty, $20,000 criminal fine
- Procurement Fraud, found guilty, fines unknown

4. Northrop Grumman
   (a) Grumman
   - Paid $2.2 million to settle allegations "that a former Grumman Data Systems vice president knowingly overstated the cost of installing a supercomputer for NASA. This settlement was in addition to a previous partial settlement of $1.1 million."
   - Kickbacks, former president received 1 year in jail (suspended), was fined $25,000, and was ordered to pay restitution of $33,000
   - False Shipping and Billing Receipts, shipping manager received three years in jail (suspended), three years probation, $50,000 fine, and had to perform 500 hours of community service
   - Conspiracy/Conversion of Classified Documents, $20,000 criminal fine, $2.5 million civil settlement, and a court assessment of $100
   - Procurement Fraud, pled guilty and received a criminal fine of $20,000
   - Fraud, $2.48 million settlement
   (b) Northrop
   - False Statement, $2.2 million civil recovery
   - False Claims/False Statements, civil settlements of $8 million, $750,000 for investigative and administrative costs, and will perform $20 million worth of corrective measures
   - Production Substitution/False Claims, $17 million fine
   - False Claims, $525,000 settlement

5. Raytheon
   - $4 million to settle allegations that the company inflated missile detection site contract prices
   - Mischarging, $3.7 million settlement
   - Defective Pricing, $2.7 million settlement
   - Conspiracy/Conversion of Classified Documents, $1 million civil and criminal settlement
   - Procurement Fraud, pled guilty, $10,000 in criminal fines

6. General Electric
   - $7.1 million settlement of a suit alleging that the company failed to satisfy electric bonding requirements for its jet engine contracts, thereby creating a safety risk
   - Misrepresentation, $2.7 million settlement
   - Money Laundering, purchase agent received thirty-nine months incarceration, three years probation, $325,222 fine, $1,950 court fees, and $324,450 in restitutions
   - Defective Pricing, $3.3 million
   - Mischarging, $576,215 reimbursement
   - Foreign Corrupt Practices Act violation, $69 million in fines, penalties, and civil damages
   - Cost Mischarging, $6.4 million settlement
   - False Claims, $1.1 million settlement
   - Defective Pricing, $8.3 million settlement, $10 million fine, and an additional $11.7 million in related civil matters. One company official received ten months in jail and a fine of $15,000. A second executive received five months in jail and a $10,000 fine.
   - Cost Mischarging, $24.6 million, voluntary disclosure
   - Defective Pricing, $900,000 settlement (Note: division since sold to Martin Marietta)

- Product substitution, $1.1 million settlement
- Conspiracy/Conversion of Classified Documents, $2.5 million civil settlement and $2.2 million in restitutions
- Procurement Fraud/Mail Fraud, $10 million criminal fine, $2.2 million in restitutions
- Fraud, $41,200 settlement, voluntary disclosure

7. Boeing
   - $75 million settlement to allegations that it had overcharged and mischarged military contracts
   - Mischarging, voluntary disclosure, $3.8 million
   - Cost Mischarging, $900,000 settlement
   - Defective Pricing, $13 million settlement
   - Conspiracy/Conversion of Classified Documents, $20,000 fine, $4 million restitution, $1 million reimbursement of investigation, $200,000 removal of overhead claims (Note: A former marketing analyst received a thirty-nine-count conviction and was jailed for a civil complaint.)

8. United Technologies
   - $150 million to settle a suit alleging that its Sikorsky Aircraft Division prematurely billed work not yet performed on a helicopter contract with the U.S. military. This settlement followed an alleged inadequate Department of Defense (DOD) voluntary disclosure.
   - Environmental Violations, penalties of $3.7 million for hazardous waste and $1.6 million for water pollution
   - Kickbacks, former purchasing agent received forty-eight months confinement, three years supervised probation, and 300 hours of community service
   - Conspiracy to Defraud, $6 million in fines

In addition, GE and Martin Marietta paid $5.87 million in January 1995 to settle a suit associated with improper sales of radar systems to Egypt. McDonnell Douglas, GM, and Hughes were all tried together for fraud and settled for $1.1 million.

With records like these, one would hope Congress might, at the very minimum, have held hearings to investigate possible defense industry criminality and have studied ways to more closely monitor the activities of the lawless contractors. Congress has not taken action to do either and is not likely to do so as long the military procurers use campaign contributions to bribe—and get protection from—those key members of Congress who benefit most from those defense industry contributions.

The Selling of Health Insurance Reform

Why do we have 41 million Americans without health-care coverage? Because they are not big campaign contributors, and those who profit from the present system are.

— FORMER SENATOR PAUL SIMON (D-IL)

It is shameful that in America—the richest of countries—more than 40 million people, many of them children, do not have health insurance. Most uninsured adults work full time but in jobs that either do not provide them with coverage or do not provide them with enough money to buy it. It simply does not make sense—practically or economically—to have so many Americans uninsured. It is important that we understand the distinction between health *care* and health *insurance*. Our health care system is the best in the world—for those who can afford it. Our health care system is not the problem. The problem is with our health insurance system. It is a disaster.

What Americans do not spend in preventive care we pay for many times over when medical emergencies hit. Highly specialized medical staff who work in hospital emergency rooms should not be spending time dispensing laxatives and aspirins. If patients delay seeing a doctor, minor ailments that could be inexpensively treated by family physicians could explode into major emergencies costing hundreds of thousands of dollars. However, when illness strikes and a routine office visit can cost a person more than he or she earns in a day, who can blame the uninsured for treating themselves instead of seeing a doctor?

Someone has to pay for the wastefulness of our system. Those who have insurance bear this burden. Very few hospitals are run as charities. Indeed, more and more community-based hospitals are being bought by private, for-profit corporations. The health care industry refers to the cost of treating those without insurance as "cost shifting." That is, the cost of treating the uninsured is shifted to the premiums that are paid by the people who are insured.

Apologists for the health insurance system status quo claim we cannot afford to insure everyone. Yet every other industrialized democracy manages to afford a system of universal health insurance. Why can't we?

Creating a system of universal health care coverage is not an impossible task. Models exist in every other Western country, so we are in a position to pick and choose from the best we see around us. We can learn what works and what to avoid. In the World Bank's 1997 international wealth survey, the United States came out on top as the richest country in the world; there is no question that we can afford health care for our citizens. But when it comes to health insurance, our country's system is inadequate and backward.

The ramifications are not strictly medical. When people miss work because they are sick yet cannot afford to see a doctor, productivity spirals down and our society suffers economically. In a global economy, our bloated, wasteful, and inefficient health insurance system hurts the overall competitiveness of our nation.

It is a scandal that we do not have an economically viable national health care system. Far worse is the fact that special interest groups have, for all intents and purposes, closed the debate. Insurance companies and their allies in managed care are calling the shots, and all those shots are aimed straight at their bottom line. The well-being of the American public no longer concerns those with the power to decide health policy for the American people.

Our inability to deal with the crisis in health insurance is intrinsically tied to the corrupting influence of campaign financing. Politicians do not seek health care solutions from ordinary voters and consumers who pay health insurance premiums. Lawmakers look to their *contributors* for advice. When it comes to health care, no one speaks for the public. No one speaks for the best interest of the nation.

The desire to effect health care reform is not a new topic. Back in 1912, Teddy Roosevelt brought up the notion of health insurance for all Americans when he was running for president as a "Bull Moose" Progressive. During the New Deal, the Committee on Economic Security issued a report calling for Social Security and a national health insurance program that would cover all Americans. Although Social Security was enacted, President Franklin D. Roosevelt abandoned the idea of universal health insurance because of opposition from the American Medical Association (AMA).

At the time, the Corrupt Campaign Practice Act of 1924 was in effect. Lyndon Johnson would later describe the act as "more loophole than law"—that is, it was totally meaningless. Consequently, there is no way of knowing whether the AMA and its health care industry allies were giving money (and if so, how much) to incumbent members of Congress or opponents of FDR's New Deal policies. There are anecdotal references to "bag men"—lobbyists for special interests—leaving paper bags full of cash for designated members of Congress. This was before my time in Congress. The campaign finance reform acts of the early 1970s at least created a system of disclosure. Now we can trace who gives and who gets campaign finance money.

President Roosevelt's successor, Harry Truman, advocated a national health insurance program, but the AMA thwarted him, too. This was during the anti-Communist McCarthy era, and rather than discussing the idea on its merits, the AMA and its allies effectively redbaited the idea of universal health care as "socialized medicine." They claimed it would make "slaves" of all American doctors.

After his landslide election in 1964, Lyndon B. Johnson succeeded in passing a publicly financed program of medical insurance for the elderly and poor. Johnson was determined to wage a "war on poverty." He knew how to twist arms to get things done, yet even he had to bow to the power of the AMA and its allies on the issue of cost control. In exchange for their support of Medicaid and Medicare, Johnson agreed to give doctors and hospitals what they wanted most—a guarantee of "cost plus" reimbursements. In order to get its support of Medicaid and Medicare, Johnson, in effect, gave the health care industry the keys to the treasury. It's no wonder that health costs soared.

When I was in Congress, cutting medical costs was a major issue. President Jimmy Carter proposed a hospital cost containment measure that challenged the ability of the medical profession to set its own rates. I voted for Carter's reform, but it did not pass. A revealing study performed by Common Cause may explain why: when Common Cause examined the relationship between votes and campaign contributions, it found those who opposed Carter's reform received four times as much money in contributions as those who supported it. The bill was defeated in the House when Richard Gephardt (D-MO) introduced a compromise bill to study the problem. When Congress votes to study rather than act on a problem, that is as good as declaring it dead.

During the time I was in Congress, Representative John Dingell (D-MI) regularly introduced a bill for national health insurance that would have, in effect, extended Medicare to all citizens. Unfortunately, his attempts to make real improvements in medical care and treatment availability were blocked by the health care industry.

Recent studies show that contributions from the health sector are sizable and continuing to increase, (The health sector, as defined by the Center for Responsive Politics for its study of industry campaign contributions, includes PACs and individuals associated with groups such as the AMA, health professionals, and the pharmaceutical industry.) In the last four election cycles, starting with 1990, the health sector has given more than $126 million to congressional candidates. In exchange for those funds, Congress never took the issue of universal health insurance seriously. It still doesn't.

Until the early 1990s, the AMA was the most active organization fighting against reform. Ironically, the AMA became the symbol of a recalcitrant health care profession. The following chart shows the financial power of the AMA, along with the amounts of money that other leading health and life insurance PACs contributed to Congress between 1979 and 1992. These figures, however, represent only a portion of the contributions because amounts of $200 or more from individuals were not included. Had large individual contributions (over $200) been included, the totals would be much higher.

American Medical Association	$14,733,596
National Association of Life Underwriters	$7,429,044
American Dental PAC	$5,828,686
Independent Insurance Agents of America	$4,188,785
American Academy of Ophthalmology	$2,622,588
American Family Life PAC	$2,461,975
American Hospital Association	$2,292,357
American Council of Life Insurance	$2,097,397

Source: *Unhealthy Money: $79 Million Buries Health Care Reform,* Part XIV, p. 6. A research report by the Citizens Fund, August 1995.

I have always admired the AMA. It's hard to believe that members of the medical profession would use their power to undermine public health. In 1994, a doctor named Steven S. Sharfstein and his son, Joshua M. Sharfstein, a statistician, published in the distinguished *New England Journal of Medicine* a study of the campaign contributions of AMPAC, the AMA's political action committee.[1]

---

1. "Campaign Contributions from the American Medical Political Action Committee to Members of Congress: For or Against Public Health?" January 6, 1994, p. 32.

The Sharfsteins uncovered facts that make me wonder whether AMA members actually know exactly where their organization is putting their money. The study identified six issues on which the AMA has taken a strong stand and compared that information with data about AMA political contributions.

The AMA, the Sharfsteins noted, has consistently—and honorably, I would add—taken a strong stand against cigarette smoking. Yet the AMA gave "significantly larger contributions to House members who favored tobacco-export promotion than to those who opposed it," the Sharfsteins reported.

In addition, while the AMA has supported the Brady Bill and other proposals for gun control, it has given more money to elect opponents of gun control than it has to proponents who support its position. When the Bush administration prohibited doctors working in federally funded clinics from discussing abortion with their patients, the AMA lobbied to have this "gag rule" repealed by Congress. The Sharfsteins found, however, that when the gag rule was in effect, the AMA's "contributions revealed a marked preference for House members who supported the gag rule over those who opposed it."

One would have expected members of the House who supported the AMA's stated public health positions on smoking, gun control, and the privileged privacy between physician and patient to have received campaign contributions to help them win re-election. Clearly, the contrary proved to be true. The AMA consistently funnelled money to members of Congress who opposed universal health insurance, regardless of where those members stood in relation to the AMA's stated positions on issues of health. Members who opposed the AMA's public health position on these three issues received an average of $13,270 from the AMA's PAC. Members who fought for health care reform received an average of $8,800 from the PAC.

We have to look at these figures carefully. The figures represent the *average*, where they may have been more useful had they reflected the *median*. Some members of Congress who opposed the AMA's position on health care issues but supported its position on health

91

insurance reform may have received $15,000 or $20,000 (decisive amounts), while others received only $1,000 or $2,000. But even the average figure has meaning. In the aggregate, it indicates that the AMA's PAC cares more about a member's position on health insurance than it does on issues concerning public health.

While I am sure there are doctors who support Senator Jesse Helms (R-NC) and many of his positions, his defense of the tobacco industry and his stand against abortion rights, gun control, and funding for AIDS research are in direct opposition to stated AMA positions on the same issues. Nonetheless, the AMA gives Helms generous financial support. In 1985–90, the AMA gave Helms $20,000. In 1991-96 he got $7,500 from the AMA (while his total from the health sector was $282,001). Why should the AMA and other health care interests give Helms any money when he is so vigorously opposed to their stated public health positions? These contributions make sense only when you realize that Helms is as vigorous in his opposition to national health insurance as he is in his opposition to AIDS research, gun control, and any legislation that threatens the profits of the tobacco industry.

The AMA does a wonderful job of promoting medical research. The organization is an excellent advocate for national health and safety. The AMA, though, tarnishes its own good reputation when it gives money to political candidates to support issues that foil the health and well-being of our nation. The Sharfstein study shows that AMA contributions are targeted at protecting its industry's economic interests and demonstrate little regard for the health of the general public.

Although Presidents Reagan and Bush had no interest in health care reform, the issue refused to die. The ability of those in the medical profession to set their own fees (which, as I said, they wrested from the Johnson administration) even when the government was paying the bill, sent costs skyrocketing across the nation. Companies that were providing health insurance as benefits to their employees wanted to find a way to trim costs and curb high premium rates. David

Broder and Haynes Johnson, in their book *The System: The American Way of Politics at the Breaking Point* (Little Brown, 1997), sum up the problem well:

> By economic terms alone, soaring health costs represented a grave threat to the nation's security and future. By the nineties, health care was consuming $1 out of every $7 of the goods and services produced in America, a higher proportion by far than any nation in the world. And those costs were rising rapidly. By the time Clinton became President, they were almost twice those of leading industrialized nations; Germans, to take one example, paid on average only half what Americans paid. . . . Every business battled rising expenses in order to provide employee health insurance, and increasing numbers of firms were compelled to reduce those benefits.

Then in 1992, Harris Wofford, a liberal Democrat and a former advisor to President John F. Kennedy, won a special election in Pennsylvania to fill the Senate seat of Republican John Heinz, who died in a plane crash. Wofford campaigned as an advocate of universal health insurance reform and his upset victory was considered a harbinger. Health care reform—really a demand for health insurance reform—suddenly became a hot issue, especially in the 1992 Democratic primary.

As health care reform grew into a prominent issue in American politics, the race for the 1992 Democratic nomination for the presidency was unfolding. Senator Bob Kerrey, a former governor of Nebraska, attempted to stake out health care reform as an issue of his own. He promoted a plan that closely resembled the single-payer system (in which the government provides health insurance) adopted by Canada and most European countries.

On the other side of the Democratic spectrum was former Massachusetts Senator Paul Tsongas (who died of cancer in 1997). Coached by a circle of academics and insurance executives who had come together in Jackson Hole, Wyoming, to discuss health care policy, Tsongas promoted an industry restructuring. His vision came to be called "managed competition" or "managed care." As Broder and Johnson reported, "The proponents of managed competition envisioned a health system relying largely on market forces of supply and demand. In this essentially private system—under which employers would pay a portion of their workers' coverage but not necessarily be required to provide the whole insurance—the government would have a limited role."

Managed care, as plotted by the Jackson Hole participants, was to be based on the growth of privately owned health maintenance organizations (HMOs) that would cut costs by streamlining service. This idea had the backing of the health care field's "Big Five" insurance companies—Cigna, Aetna, MetLife, Prudential, and The Travelers—each of which was making heavy financial investments into HMOs.

These five insurance companies had split from the industry trade association, the Health Insurance Association of America (HIAA). They were getting out of the business of traditional health indemnity insurance (the fee-for-service model of insurance), which had come to be dominated by the nonprofit Blues—Blue Shield and Blue Cross. The Big Five's strategy for regaining market share was to integrate the health care industry by placing their expertise as insurance providers alongside the healing skills of health care professionals under one profitable corporate roof.

The aftermath of the Wofford victory and the renewal of interest in health care reform resulted in an outpouring of campaign contributions. In the 1992 election cycle, health care and insurance PACs together gave a record $24.5 million to congressional candidates. Contributions from health care PACs alone represented an increase of 36 percent over the 1990 election; health sector PAC contributions rose further in the next election, totalling $16.9 million in 1994.

When discussion of health care first began, President Clinton seemed to be in favor of a universal system called the "pay-or-play" model. Businesses that did not provide health insurance for their employees would have to pay into a government fund to cover the uninsured. Once in office, Clinton abandoned pay-or-play and began to favor the managed care plan advocated by Tsongas and the Jackson Hole theorists.

President Clinton named his wife, Hillary Rodham Clinton, to lead a health care task force that would come up with a detailed proposal. Clinton bypassed Congress—and his own cabinet—and tried to keep the work of the task force behind closed doors. He clearly hoped to avoid bending to the demands of the health care industry, which, because of its campaign contributions, had a powerful hold on Congress. Clinton failed to hold off the industry and failed to achieve national health care reform.

The issue I raise here, though, is not related to the pros and cons of the Clinton effort or any other form of universal health care system. Instead, it is the amazing fact that although the single-payer option was backed by leading politicians as well as dissident medical groups such as the Association of American Physicians and Surgeons (which split off from the AMA), it was apparently never seriously considered by the Clinton task force and was dismissed without debate by a majority of Congress. The single-payer advocates had working models to point to, but they had no money to give as campaign contributions. They did not have the price of admission into the debate.

I am not a supporter of the single-payer plan, but in abandoning the single-payer idea without even bringing it up for public discussion, Clinton and members of Congress were acknowledging how money was calling the shots in the discussion of health care reform.

It would be too crude to say that the Big Five insurance companies and their HMO allies endeavored to bribe Clinton with political contributions into adopting their health care plan—the president no doubt believed that forcing Americans to join HMOs was the most viable way of providing people with some form of health care and, at the same time, cutting costs. Still, campaign contributions bought

95

access and, as it turned out, got the president's attention. Thirty-seven million dollars in health sector contributions and $15 million from insurance companies went just to congressional candidates in the 1994 elections, not to mention millions in soft money and public relations ad blitzes. There was just too much money to ignore.

Yale University Professor Ted Marmor, who has written extensively on health care reform, was one of many experts who advised Clinton on health care when Clinton was running for president. Marmor was a single-payer advocate and had sharp disagreements with advisors who opposed the single-payer solution. Broder and Johnson have described some of the deliberations that went on in Clinton's health care reform task force. After one meeting, they reported, Clinton told Marmor, "Ted, you win the debate, but I'm going with these guys," meaning the insurance companies pushing managed care. The idea of a government-run health insurance program was politically unacceptable to Clinton, who rationalized his decision by saying, "The Republicans will kill me." Even that didn't make much difference.

One of the first groups to work against "Clintoncare," as Broder and Johnson termed it, was a conservative group, Citizens for a Sound Economy. The group organized the "No Name Coalition," which brought health care businesses having a direct economic stake in the outcome of health care reform together with conservative organizations interested primarily in attacking Clinton. Broder and Johnson give a very good description of what happened. "From a handful of conservative groups, starting with the Christian Coalition," they wrote, "and the National Taxpayers Union, at times the meetings expanded to include more than thirty diverse organizations, ranging from the Health Insurance Association of America to the National Federation of Independent Business (NFIB). . . . [they] kept their conferences 'off the record' and hidden from public scrutiny. But their confirmed efforts to influence The System resulted in what became the most costly and intensively waged lobbying battle in U.S. history."

It proved to be a powerful coalition. Clinton originally thought he would benefit from the support of the big insurance companies and their corporate allies, which initially included the U.S. Chamber of Commerce. The grassroots outcry incited and mobilized by the No Name Coalition, however, turned them into opponents of any reform promoted by the Clintons. "Behind the change of direction was an intensive grassroots campaign, waged against the Chamber's national leadership by congressional Republicans and the No Name Coalition," Broder and Johnson wrote.

The Health Insurance Association of America, which represents hundreds of small insurance companies, is generally given credit for the demise of the Clinton proposal. Unlike the Big Five, the small insurance companies that had remained in the HIAA had no financial investment in HMOs and were therefore desperate to defeat the Clinton plan, which contained a strong managed-care component.

The association's notorious "Harry and Louise" advertising campaign succeeded in turning public opinion against the Clinton plan. Remember those advertisements? They depicted Harry and Louise, an imaginary middle-income couple sitting around their kitchen table discussing the details of the president's 1,364-page plan. While the advertisements were not placed in a large number of markets, the White House and Democratic National Committee reacted to them angrily. The national press, in describing the White House reaction, ran the advertisements as part of its news coverage—effectively giving the association free airtime and publicity. What Harry and Louise said was misleading at best. In one advertisement, they claimed the Clinton plan would destroy the traditional relationship between a patient and doctor—which is exactly what is happening in the health care field even with the defeat of Clinton's plan.

Willis Gradison, a nine-term congressman from Ohio and ranking minority member of the House Ways and Means Committee, exemplifies the intimate relationship between members of Congress and special interest groups like the HIAA. In January 1993, as the health care debate heated up, Gradison resigned from Congress to become chief lobbyist for the insurance industry association.

He's hardly the first lawmaker to turn lobbyist; as the Center for Public Integrity study *Beyond the Hill* showed, in a ten-year period (1984-93) 26 percent of the members who left Congress became high-paid lobbyists. However, as noted in *Beyond the Hill,* those who become lobbyists traditionally stay in office at least until their term is complete. Gradison, who had just lost an election for a Republican leadership post, could not wait. Why should he have waited? The pay as senior lobbyist is better than the pay as a member of Congress. A lobbyist with big money behind him has more influence than a member of Congress, too. As the *National Journal,* a political magazine published in Washington, characterized it, the HIAA "scored a coup in luring Gradison, who seemed likely to bring the group stature and clout with Congress and the White House."

When he became a high-powered lobbyist on health care, Gradison was in good company. Other former members of Congress, senior congressional staff, and their firms who lobbied Congress in behalf of the health care industry included

- Former senator and one-time Democratic presidential candidate Paul Tsongas. The Health Care Leadership Council hired Tsongas to lobby for a less restricted form of managed competition.

- Former Representative Thomas Downey (D-NY), my colleague on the House Ways and Means Committee. Downey started his own lobbying firm, Downey Chandler, with former Representative Rod Chandler to represent New York City-based MetLife.

- Former Representative Vin Weber (R-MN), a partner at Clark & Weinstock. He lobbied on behalf of the Alliance for Managed Care and also United Healthcare Corporation.

- Former Representative Beryl Anthony (D-AR). He lobbied for the American Hospital Association.

- Oldaker, Ryan & Leonard. This firm lobbied for the Alliance for Managed Care. Its principals include William C. Oldaker, attorney for former House Speaker Jim Wright, and Tom Ryan, a former chief aide to Energy and Commerce Committee Chairman Representative John Dingell (D-MI).
- The Ridley Group. This public relations firm headed by Timothy Ridley also worked for the Alliance for Managed Care. In 1993, Ridley hired veteran Clinton hands Gloria Cabe and David Ifshin. Cabe had been a key aide to Clinton in Little Rock, and Ifshin had worked on Clinton's presidential campaign.
- Public Strategies Washington, Inc. This firm worked for Aetna "to devise grassroots strategies," according to a spokesman. Its key employees included several former assistants to former Senator and Treasury Secretary Lloyd Bentsen.
- Deborah Steelman, a Washington attorney. Steelman was hired by both the Alliance for Managed Care and Aetna. She had formerly been a political adviser in the Bush White House where she headed a fourteen-member panel on financing health care for the uninsured.

Bill Clinton's health care plan self-destructed not only because of the amount of money invested against it or because of the number of lobbyists working against it. Clinton's plan also did not fly because, on the basis of merit, it was a lousy plan. The larger point I want to make, however, is that even a truly good reform bill—drafted by a bipartisan committee working in the open—would have been shot down by a Congress totally bought by, and beholden to, health industry money. Special interests first want to protect their own market share, not the public's health and well-being. Seduced by hefty contributions and the promise of rewards for congressional services, Congress helps them do just that.

The American people are not well served by the health care system. Too many Americans have no health insurance and cannot afford to see a doctor. In many ways we are even less well served by Congress in that it allows the debate to be distorted.

Since the defeat of the Clinton reform, Congress has passed two modest but important reform provisions. One bill allowed insured workers to take their health insurance with them when they switch jobs, while another bill extended basic insurance coverage to many uninsured children. But a comprehensive bill that would extend coverage to all Americans is dead for now. The Clinton experience was too bruising a battle. Advocates know that as long as Congress is beholden to the health insurance industry, reform is impossible. This is what I say to people who want a better health insurance system: *Push for campaign finance reform that gets special interest money out of politics.* Then and only then will our representatives be able to sit down and design a system that works for all Americans.

The Only Thing Green in Environmental Legislation Is Money

I have always considered myself a strong environmentalist. Living in and representing Hawaii—a state of great natural beauty—I could not be otherwise. I bought the first electric car in Hawaii at a time when the technology was in its infancy. I have seen the tremendous improvement in the quality of the air in Los Angeles made possible by the State of California choosing to make the catalytic converter mandatory in cars despite congressional inaction and the best efforts of the auto industry to prevent that modest but vital reform. Think of how dire the air quality of Los Angeles was not so many years ago. It seems incredible today, but the auto industry actually stood in the way of what now seems like the simplest modification in the world. At a time when their profits were sky-high, industry executives feared that people would stop buying cars if prices went up because a sure-fire piece of technology would be included in every engine so that the air would be cleaner. Just look at Los Angeles today—the point being that you *can* see it—and you'll shake your head at how stupid the whole argument was.

101

The two greatest presidents of the twentieth century were both strong environmentalists. Teddy Roosevelt was one of the first. Franklin Delano Roosevelt carried on the tradition. Environmentalism is not only concerned with preserving the beauty and the resources of our nation, it is concerned also with looking out for the health and well-being of the people of our nation.

Pollution, for example, is not just an environmental issue. It is a health issue that also involves the economy and the budget. When we allow polluting substances to foul the air, despoil the water, and poison our food we are not just affecting the quality of our lives. We are increasing medical costs. We are creating problems for future generations to clean up. We are passing along costs our children must pay.

Environmental issues, in my opinion, have become much too polarized. Environmentalists sometimes forget that people have a legitimate place in the environmental equation. Indeed, a proper understanding of ecology allows for the relationship of human beings to all other things. Were business to look at the environment from a positive perspective, it would see that creating a pollutant-free environment represents a wonderful opportunity for American industry. Unfortunately, industry is often overly concerned with generating instant profits for its shareholders. CEOs, in my opinion, would do better for their companies, the country, and the natural environment if they invested money in long-term research and development to produce products that do not despoil the world in which we live.

Projects like these obviously mean taking risks. Our country was made great by people—frontiersmen, settlers, inventors, and entrepreneurs—who had dreams and were unafraid to take risks. We need such risktakers today—people who take action and thinkers who understand that farsighted entrepreneurship is an essential part of the environmental movement.

I invested in creating the largest Spanish-language radio station in the United States, and it ultimately became a great success. That station became the top-rated station in the entire market, and it was a principal reason for my being able to increase the value of the whole radio group fivefold. Just as there was an untapped (and unappreciated) market for Spanish-language radio in Los Angeles and other parts of the country, there is an untapped and unappreciated market for environmentally friendly products from alternative energy sources to electric cars, organically grown food, chlorine-free paper, and selectively cut lumber. With a little initiative, risk taking, and support from our government, America can take the lead in manufacturing and marketing such products.

I see environmentalism not as an opposition to business prosperity but as an opportunity for business prosperity. Our industrial base could thrive again with clean, nonpolluting, high-tech products. In the same way that the government used taxpayer money to subsidize U.S. leadership in earlier technologies, we should give tax credits to companies that become pioneers in environment-friendly industries. We must view that approach not as a tax giveaway but as a sound investment for future prosperity.

Since everyone in our society benefits from clean water, pure air, and a healthy economy, there has to be a way to bring environmentalists and businesspeople to a common understanding. We need to reframe the environmental debate so that the corporate sector is willing to assume responsibility for the toxic wastes and polluting substances it produces. On the other hand, the environmental movement must accept that, instead of fighting economic development at every turn, occasional compromise with business in the quest of long-term cooperation might lead to greater progress in cleaning up our earth.

I do not believe this kind of cooperation will happen easily. As long as our political system is fueled—and polluted—by dirty money, polarization will always delineate the environmental debate.

Environmentalism is a popular issue. Poll after poll shows that the public wants a pollutant-free environment. Indeed, the popularity of environmentalism has prevented special interests from ignoring and totally overturning past environmental gains. But no matter how much support environmental organizations enjoy at the grassroots level, they do not have the money to compete effectively against corporate opponents in the campaign contribution game. Because of the amount of money available to fight environmental law, the environmental movement must play a defense game.

It used to be that an environmental "victory" meant that a good piece of legislation was passed by Congress. The creation of the Environmental Protection Agency during the Nixon Administration and, in subsequent years, the passage of the Clean Water Act, the Endangered Species Act, and the Wetlands Conservation Act were great victories for the environmental movement. But now, environmentalists tell me "victory" means that the existing legislation has been preserved, that attempts by the special interests and their congressional allies to roll back environmental protection have been defeated.

At my behest, investigative reporter Robert Schlesinger interviewed a number of pro-environment lobbyists who battle corporate lobbyists. The first thing he found was that most environmental organizations are also nonprofit organizations and therefore do not give political contributions. Those that do give have very little money to offer candidates and parties. From 1991 to 1994, combined contributions of environmentally oriented political action committees totalled $1.7 million. These relatively poorly funded PACs are pitted against a host of other industries including mining interests, the chemical industry, energy interests, forestry and paper, and automobile manufacturers. While each of these industries might have dozens of lobbyists working on one issue at a given time, an environmental organization will commonly have one lobbyist working on dozens of issues at a given time. Moreover, because environmental lobbyists do not have campaign contributions to back up their presence or their demands, they rarely spend time with members of Congress. Industry lobbyists with money behind them get appointments with members; lobbyists without money are usually relegated to meeting with legislative staffers, if that.

Corporations spend huge amounts of money to create a deregulated economic environment in which they can ignore expensive environmental measures. In the 1994 election cycle, for example, chemical manufacturers—including manufacturers of pesticides, herbicides, and other toxic agrochemicals—gave congressional candidates more than $3.7 million. The oil/gasoline and natural gas industries gave $11.3 million. Electric utilities gave $4.4 million. The forestry and paper product industry gave $2.2 million. Mining companies gave almost $1.7 million. Waste management companies gave $1.2 million. These millions are spent for one purpose: to foster legislation that encourages economic growth at the expense of environmental protection.

When a group lobbying for one side of an environmental issue is plying members of Congress with money for re-election but lobbyists on the other side have nothing but the weight of their arguments to offer, a reasonably objective discussion is impossible. In that sort of extreme situation, how can the two sides sit down with members of Congress and dispassionately discuss an issue in terms of the national interest, in terms of what is best for the people? Let me be clear: I equate protecting the environment with protecting the national interest. I am convinced that succeeding in both requires campaign finance reform. We must get special interest money out of politics. Only then will legislators and lobbyists on all sides of an issue be able to debate the issue on its merits and as equals.

Curtis Moore, a former Republican counsel on the Senate Environment and Public Works Committee, is now a Washington lawyer and lobbyist. In William Greider's excellent 1992 book, *Who Will Tell the People: The Betrayal of Democracy*, Moore described the way campaign contributions affect legislation on environmental issues. "If I represent an industry, I can always get into an argument in the Executive Branch or in Congress by the nature of the fact that I have money," Moore said. "But if you're an environmental group, you can't get into the argument unless they want to let you in." As Moore explained it, "they" in this context refers to the lobbyists who buy access to legislators and their aides and who use their access to frame the terms of debate and the intent of the pending legislation.

Environmentalist lobbyists who do not accept those terms are considered to have nothing positive to contribute and, with no input into the discussion, have no influence on the way the legislation is drafted.

When I was in Congress, President Carter, who understood energy technology, promoted the research and development of alternative energy sources. Carter introduced a tax credit for individuals and companies that installed solar heating, wind power, and other alternative energy sources. This is the kind of tax subsidy I would favor—that is, if there were a place for tax subsidies at all. The tax credit for alternative energy did not go to gigantic corporations that did not need it. Instead, it went to forward-looking consumers who created a demand that benefitted inventive entrepreneurs who were willing to take risks to be on the cutting edge of new technology. But the alternative energy companies lacked the resources to make huge donations to Congress. In 1994, for example, their combined contributions to Congress totalled just $45,269.

Had solar and wind power—encouraged by government policy—been allowed to prosper, then clean, safe, domestic energy would have been produced. Jobs would have been produced, too. In the long run, this new industry would have repaid tax credits with its own tax payments. Thanks to Carter's support, the alternative energy industry boomed for a brief period. It almost seemed that America would break its dependence on foreign oil sources. That would have been a good thing for many reasons, one being that a good deal of the military budget went to protecting foreign oil sources. I was proud of supporting President Carter on alternative energy.

President Reagan, with the compliance of a Congress dependent on money from oil, gas, nuclear, and coal-producing industries, took the tax credit away from alternative producers while he maintained expensive subsidies for environmentally hazardous nuclear and fossil fuel energy producers—the companies that made big campaign contributions. According to Taxpayers for Common Sense, subsidies to the fossil fuel industry exceed $5 billion per year. Cut those subsidies, and clean energy sources would become much more competitive.

Alternative energy is a good idea and the hope of the future. But without government support—and without the financial resources to bribe legislators into giving it support—the industry cannot grow. The decision to support fossil and nuclear energy at the expense of clean energy sources violated common-sense thinking. Even if I'm wrong, the debate on the issue was, at best, distorted by money.

Big industry buys a lot of legislation with its campaign money. Corporate donors know whom to give their money to, and from the standpoint of their own return on investment, they have been very successful in their choices.

Seventeen of the top twenty recipients of timber PAC contributions in the House voted against a 1992 amendment that would have cut $18 million for timber preparation and road construction in roadless areas of our national forests. Those voting against the amendment received 72 percent of all timber PAC contributions that went to House members in 1992. That amount represents almost three times more than amendment supporters received.

In 1993, in shaping the final version of The Department of Energy National Security Act, campaign contributions had more influence than rational debate about national priorities. On four key votes about crucial environmental issues—global warming, nuclear licensing, automobile mileage standards, and oil drilling in the Arctic National Wildlife Refuge—the Senate Energy Committee adopted the position of the energy industry over the opposition of environmental and consumer organizations. Between 1985 and 1991, members of the Senate Energy Committee received over $3 million in contributions from 187 energy industry PACs concerned with those four issues.

Another example of the powerful role campaign contributions play in environmental issues involves the Comprehensive Mining Reform bill of 1993. That bill was a belated attempt to reform the Mining Law of 1872, a boon to private mining companies. Under the terms of the 1872 law, mining companies could extract minerals— gold, silver, and copper—from publicly owned land for free. They did not have to pay royalties to the federal government, although they were required to pay royalties of up to 22 percent on some state and private lands. The old law also let mining companies buy public land for $2.50 to $5.00 an acre, a price that reflects costs in 1872, not today's fair market value.

The 1872 law gives mining companies enormous tax breaks, too. Companies mining on public lands can deduct the annual value of their extracted minerals, a program known as the "percentage deple-tion allowance." It works like this: if gold being mined from public lands is estimated at a value of $100 million, a mining company can deduct the value of what it mined—say, $10 million for each tax year—from its taxes. Minerals are viewed as private assets that belong to the company even though the mine might be on public land owned, in theory, by the public. If you add up the hard-rock minerals and the depletion allowance that fossil fuel companies also extract from the government, you will find that the U.S. Treasury loses about $2.4 bil-lion a year because of these tax breaks. For the extraction industry, those tax savings represent a very nice return on its investment.

Common sense again, and elemental fairness, would dictate that the mining companies pay a royalty to the public. Mining occurs in a few sparsely settled western states. The congressional delegations from those states represent a small minority. Wouldn't it follow that the majority of legislators representing the rest of the country would oppose the giveaways mining moguls receive as a result of the 1872 law? Shouldn't these legislators be interested in generating revenue for the U.S. Treasury? The mining industry wields a lot of financial clout in the halls of Congress. When it comes to reforming outdated spe-cial interest legislation, money often means more than common sense.

Anna Aurilio, a staff scientist at U.S. Public Interest Research Group (USPIRG), told Schlesinger, "The mining industry is very strategic. They give their campaign contributions to the heads of the resources committees, the relevant authorizing committees." For example, the senators who cosponsored the failed reform bill that would have overturned the 1872 law received, on average, one-tenth as much money from mining PACs as senators who cosponsored an industry-backed bill that passed in the Senate. Aurilio added, "When I go to Ways & Means Committee people or when I suggest closing that loophole as a way of raising revenues, people just . . . it's like, 'What, are you nuts?'. . . It can't be done, just because of the opposition." And what they mean is that there is just too much money at stake on the vote. The mining industry has given big money to too many members of Congress. One return on that investment is the way the members vote.

Aurilio lobbied for reform, but the industry won; it kept the status quo and the royalties. The industry made an investment of approximately $1.1 million and $1.7 million, respectively, to congressional candidates in the 1992 and 1994 elections, as the issue was being debated. For that investment, the hard-rock mining industry pocketed approximately $200 million per year in royalties. Had the Comprehensive Mining Reform bill of 1993 passed, every year that $200 million would have gone into the U.S. Treasury and helped reduce the deficit. The issue generated very little political debate or media coverage, except in those few western states where hard-rock mining is an important economic activity.

The only revision that public interest groups have managed to get from the 1872 Mining Law is a moratorium on the practice of granting land patents, i.e., selling off public lands. Mining companies are still exempt from all environmental regulations. They are free to extract as much gold as possible and leave a mess for the public to clean up.

Both political parties are responsible. Pork-barrel politics is not a partisan issue. When both parties were arguing about which could be better trusted to cut the deficit, Congress voted for, and the president approved, a bill that would give the oil industry (which does pay royalties) a holiday from their royalties as an incentive for deep-water drilling in the Gulf of Mexico. "Clearly, it's not partisan either, all this pork stuff, it's nonpartisan," Aurilio said. "Both sides love it. They both get lots of money from the bad guys and it's outrageous."

The buying of our natural resources continues no matter who is president or which party controls Congress. In 1996, a presidential election year, ARCO, the Atlantic Richfield Company, contributed $1,250,843 in soft money, $486,372 of it to the Democrats. It also gave a substantial amount of money, $255,343, to individual congressional candidates; some 83 percent went to Republicans. In 1994, ARCO contributed $288,493—59 percent to Republicans. It should now be obvious what questions follow: Why did ARCO contribute so much money? What did it expect to get in the way of a payback?

ARCO is one of the principal oil companies drilling in Alaska's North Slope. When this vast, ecologically fragile wilderness area was first opened to oil drilling, the idea was to help our country's energy independence. Congress opened the area to oil drilling and allowed the construction of the Trans-Alaska oil pipeline only on the condition that the oil be used for domestic purposes. Though the pipeline has consistently leaked oil and the *Exxon Valdez* oil spill was an ecological disaster, Alaskan oil served to keep oil prices down and lessen, though not eradicate, our dependence on Middle East oil (for which taxpayers pay a huge price in military protection). Under President Clinton, though, the restriction on oil exports was lifted. North Slope oil now flows through the Arctic pipeline into ships headed to Japan, South Korea, Taiwan, and China. Oil exports not only fatten the profits of ARCO and other producers, but they reduce our domestic reserves and cause upward pressure on domestic prices, which also profits the Alaskan producers.

There is no defensible reason for either Congress or the president to sanction these oil exports. The issue is a "no-brainer." Expanding oil production in a fragile area and exporting a precious nonrenewable natural resource is against the interests of the American people. It is against the long-term security of the American nation. The bill passed, but not because of arguments ARCO made to defend the exports. It happened because of money—the million-plus dollars in campaign contributions that ARCO gave.

No matter what the issue--waste management, energy, forestry, grazing on public lands, logging in national forests, digging for coal, or drilling for oil—campaign contributions from rich and powerful special interest groups dictate public policy. Conserving our natural resources and protecting the environment require campaign finance reform that gets money out of politics. A rational, common-sense, people-first, pro-American environmental policy requires rational debate among political equals who agree the national interest is their top priority.

CHAPTER TEN

The Auto Industry

Government spending attracts special interests like bears to honey, and it has been this way since the earliest days of our country. Through much of the nineteenth century, government assistance was held out as an inducement to encourage the construction of public works—canals, roads, courthouses, post offices, and other federal buildings. Even back then, political payola greased the process of contract-letting.

Today, it is the auto industry that wields financial power. As the nineteenth century railroads once did, now the auto industry uses its wealth to win special favors, regardless of the effect they have on the American public. The auto industry generally carries on with a public-be-damned attitude that has had a disastrous impact on the nation's development and the entire planet's natural environment.

Having had my own run-in with General Motors, I know first-hand about the power it wields over members of Congress. In 1983, while still in Congress, I was badly injured in a one-car crash in Washington. The brakes on my brand new Oldsmobile Cutlass Sierra failed. I was heading toward the Kennedy Center from the Capitol at about three o'clock in the afternoon on a lovely tree-lined road along the Tidal Basin, a little south of the White House. Cars began slowing down ahead of me. I was going about thirty miles an hour. I tried to slow down but could not. I pumped the brake pedal and got no resistance from the pedal. My foot went straight down to the floor. I kept pumping the brake. Nothing happened. As I pumped, I turned the steering wheel as sharply as I could to avoid ramming into the car in front of me.

Miraculously, I got over a curb and out of traffic. That is when my luck ran out. The Olds, gliding too fast, smashed into a 150-year-old tree.

I had been totally rigid, arms taut, as I tried to avoid the collision. The result was broken bones and numerous other injuries. My left hip was shattered. It took a series of plates and pins and one of the most skillful hip surgeons in the country to rebuild it. My right ankle and heel were almost useless. I met with seven orthopedic specialists who thought they could not repair the damage, but my eighth doctor, Dr. William Wagner, then of Whittier, California, was not afraid to operate and fuse solid the joints of my ankle. He put me on a regimen of strenuous physical therapy and said recovery would be a long, hard process. It was, but after eight years of therapy I was able to walk with no apparent limp.

As a result of this accident I became curious about General Motors—indeed, about the whole automobile industry. I began to investigate and discovered an interesting, and suspect, flaw in the Traffic Safety Act of 1966. The flaw exempted automobile executives from criminal prosecution for knowingly building cars with potentially fatal construction or design defects. As the 1966 law was written, executives are exempt from criminal charges no matter how culpable the evidence shows them to be. The Traffic Safety Act arbitrarily exempts automobile executives for assuming responsibility for unsafe cars. No other industry or profession has such explicit, blanket immunity from criminal prosecution.

In the Senate debate over the 1966 act, Vance Hartke, an Indiana Democrat with a reputation for being the consumer's friend, pushed to have the legislation include civil and criminal penalties so as to punish willful, and therefore avoidable, safety violations. One of the industry's allies, John Pastore, a Rhode Island Democrat with no

General Motors manufacturing plants in his state, responded emotionally. Pastore defended auto manufacturers and said it would be "obnoxious" to subject their executives to criminal actions for safety violations.

"We are not dealing with mobsters and gangsters," Pastore said. "We are dealing with an industry that is the industrial pride of America.... I can say for General Motors, for Chrysler, and I can say for the Ford Motor Company, that they are not willfully and deliberately going to refuse to put a safety device on an automobile."

Hartke accurately noted that if there were no willful violations, the auto companies would have nothing to worry about. Yet his amendment was overwhelmingly defeated: 62 votes against, 14 in favor, 24 (an extraordinarily large number) not voting. The absent senators—unwilling to vote against the Hartke bill and take a position they conscientiously could not abide, yet unwilling to buck the auto industry by supporting the Hartke bill—simply sat out the vote. It was a senatorial sell out.

The defeat of Hartke's bill exempted auto industry executives from any liability for dangerous products. Even if there were a video tape of GM's board of directors ordering engineers to design the cheapest possible vehicle, regardless of the number of deaths that shoddy construction might cause, it would not matter. They could not be punished by criminal sanctions.

Of course, auto executives engage in that kind of cost and safety planning all the time. Let's say auto executives are mulling over the cost/benefit analysis of an unsafe innovation. They estimate that the innovation might boost profits by $100 million. On the other hand, they surmise, people might die and so the company might have to pay victims' families around $10 million. Based on those numbers, the decision would be a no-brainer for the executives concerned only with the financial bottom line: to hell with safety; go for the profits.

This explains the industry's historical reluctance to install seat belts, airbags, and other consumer safety features. Yes, I know, cars now have seat belts and airbags as standard safety features, but only because of consumer pressure, the efforts of consumer advocates to make safety a political issue. Left to itself, the auto industry would give safety features low priority.

Did campaign contributions affect the outcome of the vote on the Traffic Safety Act? Did the auto industry get its way because of political payola? We will never know. Disclosure laws for campaign finance were so flimsy in 1966 that there is no accurate record documenting special interest campaign contributions to members of Congress.

Nevertheless, it is interesting to compare the attitude of Congress, where campaign funds are needed, with the attitude of the judiciary. Because they are appointed, federal judges do not need to raise money for their elections. Congress, dependent on auto industry campaign contributions, allows the industry to get away with murder. The courts, seemingly free of political payola and therefore more independent, force industry to pay for its irresponsibility.

Recent litigation underscores the point. On December 20, 1996, a Louisiana judge approved a class action settlement in a civil suit. The settlement gave $10,000 certificates good toward the purchase of a new vehicle to 5.8 million owners of GM pickup trucks with side-mounted gas tanks. If 25 percent of the owners redeem the certificates, GM's payout will be almost $1.5 billion. In addition, the judge ordered GM to pay $28 million in legal fees and expenses—the maximum.

The main point is this: Congress created a situation in which the auto manufacturers can get away with killing people and, literally, not have to face criminal prosecution.

After my accident and subsequent discovery of the exemption the auto industry bought for itself in the 1966 Traffic Safety Act, I drew up legislation that would have made the auto industry accountable for its products, just like other industries. I submitted the bill to a consumer protection subcommittee of the House Energy and Commerce Committee, which seemed the proper place for it.

I was not a member of that committee, but subcommittee Chairman Tim Wirth, then a Democratic representative from Colorado, agreed to move the bill. He warned me that Michigan's John Dingell (D), the full committee chairman, would never let my bill see the light of day. Wirth was right.

Wirth's subcommittee approved the legislation, which then went directly into Dingell's hands. Dingell has been a powerful force in Congress. In many ways, he is a fine public servant. He has fought hard for a decent health care system and health insurance reform, but when it comes to the automobile industry, he is in General Motors's pocket. As the representative from Detroit, where GM is headquartered, this is not surprising. GM represents the interests of voters in Dingell's district, so GM does not have to ply Dingell with money. Auto companies do, however, give money to other members of Congress. In the 1994 election cycle, car companies gave $414,440 to members sitting on the House Transportation Committee (of which Dingell received $28,000).

As far as my legislation was concerned, Dingell went through the motions. His committee held a hearing on it and one member of the staff invited me. Also invited were eight or ten industry lobbyists who did not merely watch but actively participated in the hearing. The lobbyists were going over the details of my bill with Dingell's staff, and together, they were developing strategies to defeat the bill. Dingell was not there, but his chief of staff was. When I tried to join the discussion, the chief of staff came up to me and said, "You were not invited to this hearing by the chairman or by me."

So here was the spectacle of a member of Congress—one whose bill was being debated, no less—ousted from a hearing, not by the chair of the committee or even another member of Congress, but by a staff aide! Meanwhile, industry lobbyists, representing a special interest with money (as opposed to a public interest group with constituents) were not only allowed to attend the hearing, they were encouraged to participate in the discussion.

Whose Congress is it? The people's or the lobbyists' and those who pay them? To me this was stunning proof of who runs the legislative process. I, a member of Congress elected by the people of Hawaii, could not participate in a discussion of a bill that I myself had drafted, while lobbyists were invited to help kill the bill. It's obvious to me that in government, he who pays the piper calls the tune. The interest groups that finance politicians wield power over the politicians. The lobbyists are on the scene—in Congress—to make sure that the members *know* they have the power. And what about the voters back home? Their attention is absorbed by the ups and downs of everyday life. There's no way for them to keep track of what their representatives are doing or to pay attention to legislative detail. So the special interest groups, and the lobbyists who represent them, end up as partners—paying partners—to politicians in running the country.

This may be the way government works, but it is not the way it ought to be. I called Dingell to protest my silencing but got no satisfaction. "That aide was representing me," he said. "You were not invited by me and you had no place there."

Chairman Dingell's opposition assured the defeat of my legislation. Committee members who go against committee chairs risk forfeiting the leadership's support for their own bills. That's how independent members are punished. Powerful committee chairmen like Dingell play a game of punishment and reward and can also direct contributions to those members who are willing to play their game.

John Dingell is neither a bad person nor a bad member of Congress. In matters aside from those dealing with the auto industry, he has been an effective, fair-minded legislator: serious, knowledgeable, and unafraid to challenge powerful forces. He throws his weight around and people fear him, but when he fights for issues, he usually takes the side of the public good.

Dingell entered Congress in 1955, taking the seat that had been his father's for many years. In 1943, the elder Dingell became the first member of Congress to propose national health insurance. Like father, like son: the junior Dingell introduced the same bill for national health insurance year after year. In 1993 and 1994, he embraced President Clinton's health care plan but could not get Clinton's bill out of committee due to pressure from the insurance industry.

Something is obviously wrong, but the flaw is not with individual members' ethics. The flaw is with the institutional dependence on money. Even though I was a member of Congress, I was dead in the water when auto industry lobbyists were against me. In the same way, when health insurance lobbyists were against Dingell, he was dead in the water. No matter which committee is involved, the shots get called by the lobbyists representing contributors and by the members of Congress who take donations from those contributors. The public is as powerless as members who oppose monied interests.

The experience I had with Dingell's House Energy and Commerce Committee gave me insight into the coziness between key legislators and special interest lobbyists. The rule is this: In any clash between the public interest and special interests, the special interests will prevail. They provide the money that elects members of Congress. Voters, who know very little about what goes on behind the scenes in Congress, do not get heard.

I ended up suing GM over my auto accident. That was no picnic either. GM's lawyers kept up a steady stream of delays, side issues, and costly legal maneuvering. The average person does not have the resources to finance such a fight. I was lucky enough to have had the means and the inclination. After several years, even I decided enough was enough. GM paid me on the condition I not reveal the nature and amount of the settlement. I will honor that agreement here.

The auto manufacturers are only one part of the problem. Used-car dealers, because they too give campaign contributions to influential legislators, also dictate congressional policy. In the late 1970s, the Federal Trade Commission (FTC) formulated rules requiring used-car dealers to reveal defects in the cars on their lot. This was one of those common-sense consumer protection rules that should not have caused controversy. I supported the regulations as, at first, did most members of Congress. Used-car dealers who buy a defective car ought to alert prospective buyers to the defects in the car, or they should repair the defects before putting the car up for sale.

In 1980, the dealers responded by pressing legislators to pass a law that gave Congress the ability to veto the FTC rules. The National Auto Dealers Association (NADA) was a relatively small PAC until this time. When I first entered Congress in 1977, it gave $368,000 to 270 candidates. In 1980, while lobbying for this rule, its contributions exceeded $1 million for the first time.

In 1982, consumer-oriented members of Congress tried to fight back and attempted to pass legislation based on the FTC regulation. The so-called Lemon Law would have made dealers responsible for selling cars they knew to be "lemons," that is, containing some kind of hidden damage. Knowing my colleagues in the House, I believe most of them sympathized with the purpose of this bill, and I am certain it would have passed easily were it not for NADA's contributions, which totalled $2,351,925 in the 1995-96 cycle. The Lemon Law proposal was defeated by a vote of 69 to 27 in the Senate. In the House, the vote was 286 to 133. A colleague in the House explained the defeat of the popular, pro-consumer bill to *New Yorker* columnist Elizabeth Drew. "Of course it was money," the congressman told Drew. "Why else would they vote for used-car dealers?" (Elizabeth Drew, *Politics and Money: The New Road to Corruption*, Macmillan, 1983, p. 78. Note: The member of Congress was not named in the article.)

NADA money rolled over Congress. Ninety percent of the members who received more than $4,000 from NADA voted against the bill. Of the members who got from $1,000 to $3,000 from NADA, 88.3 percent supported NADA and opposed the bill. Only 34.2 percent of those who got nothing from NADA agreed with NADA's point of view.

Professor Larry Sabato, a political scientist at the University of Virginia, studied this issue. He reported that in 1982, of the 251 legislators who voted against the Lemon Law and ran for re-election, 89 percent received an average of $2,300 each from NADA.

Averages can be deceptive. I would never suggest that a campaign contribution of $2,300 would buy a legislator's vote. The relation of votes to money is more complex than that. An *average* includes contributions that are both higher and lower. Moreover, when the threat of that amount going to an opponent is factored in, a contribution's value doubles. Contributions worth $5,000 or $10,000 begin to have weight. Members of Congress are in a tough position. They can either take money from a group that wants to control their vote, or they can go out and raise money from the public, which is time-consuming and usually not as lucrative.

Had members of Congress listened to the voters instead of listening to the used-car dealers and pocketing their money, would they have opposed the Lemon Law? Just how much do campaign contributions count?

One answer to these questions might be found in the decisions of our courts. Unlike legislators (and presidents), federal court judges are not allowed to take money from the lawyers and the defendants who come before them. It would be bribery.

In chapter 1, I described how members of Congress have exempted themselves from the crime of bribery. It's an observation that, though obvious, bears repeating. If a lawyer representing an interest group in a judicial proceeding were to offer the judge a sum of money, that lawyer would be arrested for bribery. But were that same lawyer to have an interest in an issue before Congress, he or she could give members of Congress deciding that issue thousands of dollars and it would not be bribery. It would be a perfectly legal campaign contribution. It's no wonder then that the judiciary overturned Congress's complicit agreement with the used-car dealers. In 1982, a U.S. Court of Appeals ruled that a legislative veto of an FTC regulation violates the separation of powers and is unconstitutional.

The auto industry has always put profits before safety and before environmental protection. It fought airbags and seat belts. It fights all safety measures, all consumer measures, all energy-saving measures, all measures that cut pollution and preserve the environment. The only reason American cars got better was because tough Japanese and European competition forced the industry to improve products or sacrifice profits. Foreign competition forced American automakers to a new standard far above that of the rattletraps that, like the Corvair exposed by Ralph Nader, were "unsafe at any speed."

The auto industry could cut gasoline consumption, but it lacks the will. Government has the power to set standards and force the auto industry to comply, but too many key legislators are dependent on the auto and oil industries for their campaign dollars. Public Citizen, a consumer group founded by Ralph Nader, estimates that consumers now save more than $3,000 at the gas pump over the course of a new car's life because government regulations, on top of Japanese competition, forced automakers to produce better engines.

If not for German and Japanese technology that gave Americans what they wanted—cars that got good gas mileage—American car manufacturers would have had no incentive to improve engine performance. Without the Japanese imports, American automakers would still be producing gas-guzzling engines. When American car buyers started buying Japanese, though, the domestic auto industry responded fast. Between 1975 and 1985, fuel economy in this country doubled, saving consumers billions of dollars and reducing the country's dependence upon foreign oil. In 1975, Congress accelerated this trend by introducing Corporate Average Fuel Economy (CAFE) standards over the bitter opposition of the American automakers. CAFE made it mandatory for American automakers to meet Japanese standards of gas consumption. The fact that American carmakers were able to respond so quickly indicates that they already had the technology to cut fuel consumption. It took foreign competition and government regulations to force them into doing it.

It is worth noting that foreign and American carmakers have learned some tricks—both good and bad—from each other. Taken to task by the Japanese, American carmakers figured out how to cut gas consumption. On the flip side of the coin, foreign carmakers figured out how to win favors by investing in Congress. In the 1994 election, two PACs representing Japanese import dealers contributed more than $1 million to congressional candidates. NADA (the PAC representing American auto dealers, some of whom also sell foreign cars) contributed $1.8 million. GM, Ford, and Chrysler gave another $1.2 million. In the 1996 elections, PAC contributions from NADA totalled $2.3 million; GM, $310,475; Ford, $343,590; and Chrysler, $304,615.

Just as auto companies have successfully bribed Congress to protect them from taking responsibility for their mistakes, they, along with the petroleum industry, have bribed Congress into exempting them from environmental controls. More than 25 years since the first Earth Day, the auto industry, along with its oil company friends, remain the principal obstacle to fighting the greenhouse effect and combating global climate change.

Scientists agree that automobile emissions are the single largest source of greenhouse gas emissions in the country. More efficient cars would lower gas consumption and, with that, oil company profits. The oil and gas industry, which in 1994 gave $8.9 million to congressional candidates, resists greater efficiency. Though it would be in the national interest to cut our dependence on foreign oil, the government continues to give the oil industry tax relief to drill for oil that America would not need if gas mileage standards were raised.

When Jimmy Carter was president, he proposed a ten-cents-per-gallon tax on gasoline in an effort to encourage conservation. I was among the 7 or 8 percent in Congress to vote in favor of it. My sense of outrage was so great, I introduced a bill calling for a fifty-cents-per-gallon tax. Of course, it never saw the light of day in Washington, but it did earn me a primary election opponent in Hawaii during the next campaign who ran solely on that issue. (I won with only 73 percent of the vote.) I did get invited—once—to speak on the issue. It was in Germany at a newspaper editors' conference. That's how much interest and chance there was for such an idea to become reality in the face of special interest oil industry opposition.

Actually, the term "foreign oil" is a misnomer. American oil companies are involved in drilling for oil all over the world. Sometimes the companies own the oil fields, sometimes the country in which they are located owns them, but the American companies do the actual drilling. Whether the oil fields are nationalized or privatized, American oil companies are often involved in drilling and transport. American military policy is formulated to protect the investments of these companies. An honest accounting of oil's cost to the consumer would include the hundreds of billions of dollars we taxpayers pay for military protection.

I believe that our government should protect American business investment overseas. But we should do it only on the basis of national self-interest, not because the oil companies, through their campaign contributions, have bribed politicians to do their bidding. Moving away from oil dependence would be good for the country. It would allow us to cut military spending, it would do wonders for the environment, and it might also encourage new high-tech, environment-friendly, safe-energy businesses. Detroit's insistence on building oversized gas guzzlers (and the public's passion for driving the same) is a major factor in our polluted air, our bloated debt, and our budget deficit.

As a presidential candidate in 1992, Bill Clinton talked about how he would raise fuel economy standards for cars and light trucks, thus lowering fuel emissions and oil dependence. Clinton also knew whom to thank for his campaign contributions. In the 1996 election cycle, the auto industry gave $500,500 and the oil and gas industry gave $2.7 million to the Democratic party in soft money alone.

During Clinton's first term in office, the auto industry twice successfully pressured Congress to defeat higher fuel economy standards. During the 1996 election cycle, the automotive industry gave $8.8 million to political candidates, 77 percent of which went to members of the Republican party, the majority in Congress.

123

Rather than challenge big money interests like the auto manu-facturers, Clinton, as he so often does, surrendered to them. Consequently, the plan he finally introduced did not have any fuel economy standards for automobiles. Ultimately, Clinton proposed to give the auto industry $500 million to create a consortium called "Partnership for a New Generation of Vehicles." The consortium was charged with developing one prototype gas-efficient car. Thanks to the money Clinton set aside for them, the auto industry will not have to use its own plentiful resources to do something that good old-fashioned American enterprise should have done in the first place. But in formulating this policy, Clinton was more attentive to the needs of the auto industry than he was to his own common sense and the needs of the nation.

I was personally pleased when, in 1994, the Democrats were defeated and lost their control of Congress. As I have insisted, the potential for political corruption is built into the institution of Congress. After forty years in power, the Democrats had become part of the institution. They had become entrenched and arrogant with power. The House needed to be swept clean.

The Republicans who came to power were not much different from the Democrats who lost power. They, too, used their incumbency to raise campaign contributions. Thus, in 1996, PACs representing automobile manufacturers and dealers gave the Republican party $1.8 million. To help the auto industry sell more high-priced cars, the Republican-controlled Congress phased out the luxury tax on cars that sell for more than $34,000. The tax will be reduced 1 percent a year until the year 2003, when it will disappear altogether. This means that expensive gas guzzlers will be cheaper to buy. Pollution from these cars is greater than it is from less expensive cars that are smaller and lighter. But the auto industry makes more profit from the gas guzzlers. It's therefore not surprising that those members of Congress who are supported by auto industry money are going to support industry demands regardless of their effect on the environment.

Campaign contributions reflect a hidden history of our country. Contributions from the transportation industry have affected more than the construction of railroads and highways. They have affected how the country was settled and our system of democratic majority rule, as well as issues of race, civil rights, public health and safety, and the environment. Indeed, when one contemplates the effect on the environment of auto pollutants, the campaign contributions given by the auto industry affect humanity and the very future of the earth.

Those who give campaign contributions in behalf of one industry or another do not have the big picture in mind. What motivates their giving is not the future of the planet or the health and well-being of the public. What motivates them is the profitability of their single enterprise. I do not condemn them for their narrow concern. Lobbyists work for corporations, corporations are owned by shareholders, and everyone has a right to make a profit.

Democracy, however, should mean more than simply making a buck. That people can govern themselves is a grand enterprise, the greatest experiment in all the world. In that respect, politics embraces more concerns than mere economics. It's about humanity, the earth; as Thomas Jefferson so nobly put it, it's about "life, liberty, and the pursuit of happiness." That is why we need to get special single-interest money out of politics. Dollars should not be the determining factor in our democracy. Politics should be about programs and ideas decided on the basis of merit rather than money. What's good for the nation and the people is what counts. Special interests should have a role in the democratic process, but they should not be able to own or buy the system. They should be a *part* of the discussion and debate, *just like everyone else.*

CHAPTER ELEVEN

My Call for Reform

Many people are going to ask, How are we going to get meaningful, comprehensive reform if even the most token efforts at reforming the campaign finance system are stymied by Congress?

Given the pathetic record of the 105th Congress, which would not even endorse the well-intended but essentially weak McCain-Feingold proposal, that is a very good question.

I have great respect for Senators Russ Feingold (D-WI) and John McCain (R-AZ), who formulated a bill that they believed would incorporate the minimum provisions for reform that would be acceptable to their colleagues. I admire Senator McCain for bucking his party's leadership in pushing his bill. Russ Feingold, too, has promoted reform even when his own party did not want it. During the first two years of the Clinton administration, when the Democrats controlled Congress, Feingold advocated campaign finance reform, but the leaders of his party would not have it. Republicans and Democrats act the same when they are the majority party. Why overhaul a system that gave them control of Congress? Although the Republicans are to blame for the defeat of reform in the 105th Congress, the Democrats share their shame.

There are, however, a growing number of senators and representatives who, like McCain and Feingold, really want to improve the system. But they are still a minority. For the majority, campaign finance reform remains a partisan issue, a way to embarrass the other party, a cynical means of sounding self-righteous while doing nothing.

The McCain-Feingold bill had flaws that contributed to its defeat in Congress. First of all, it was not real reform; it was cosmetic in concept. Its principle provision, a ban on soft money, is an essential part of any reform. And to give Senators McCain and Feingold credit, their initial draft of the bill would have banned soft money and placed voluntary limits on the amount of hard money individual candidates could spend in an election. But in order to win support from the many hypocrites in Congress, they had to water down their bill and give up on spending limits. In so doing, they undercut the purpose of their own bill. Had McCain-Feingold passed, the money that now goes to political parties as soft money would in the future go directly to political candidates as hard money. That's not a reform. It simply changes the channel of political giving without limiting the power of the economic elite to maintain their control of the political process.

In order to assure that even so meaningless a bill would not pass, the Republicans prepared an amendment that would have essentially destroyed labor's ability to give any campaign contributions. Republicans make a big deal of the amount of money labor unions give to the Democratic party. What they don't say is that business interests typically give *eleven times* as much (for example, business gave roughly $653 million in 1996; labor, $58 million), most of which goes to Republicans in hard and soft money. Just as labor unions give money to candidates without actually polling its members, corporations give money to candidates without consulting their shareholders, their employees, or the people who buy their products.

The whole system is rotten. To restrict labor unions in making political contributions while allowing corporations to continue their giving is palpably unfair and antidemocratic. But, of course, the Republicans weren't serious about this proposal. They knew that if restrictions on unions were included in the McCain-Feingold

127

package, Democrats—traditionally supported by labor—would have voted against it. Republicans believed that they could then blame Democrats for the defeat of campaign finance reform in this session.

The cynicism of those who oppose campaign finance reform appalls me. I have no faith that Congress will ever pass campaign finance reform unless the public demands it and shows itself willing to toss out of office those who stand against it.

We, the people, *must* let Congress know we are not just fed up, we are boiling angry. We *must* bring public opinion to bear. I have seen how members react when faced with an active, angry citizenry. People are usually too busy with job and family responsibilities to focus their attention on Congress. That is why lobbyists, who can focus on issues and are backed by campaign contributions, can wield so much power. But *when the public gets active and gets excited about an issue, politicians take notice.*

Nothing terrifies members of Congress more than a mass of irate voters. As a people, we must use our voting power to show elected officials that we will not stand for them selling off our government to the highest bidders. With our votes we must show them the penalty for campaign extortion and bribery: they will get sent back home, if not to jail.

This is a message politicians understand. As Fred Thompson, the Republican senator from Tennessee, said in a 1996 *Washington Post* interview, "Someone will be defeated for opposing campaign finance reform, or it will be perceived that way, and then we'll all [start taking] notice."

I believe that a movement for meaningful campaign finance reform must start at the state level, where it's easier for people to wield direct political power, where it's easier for citizens to vote politicians out of office, where it's easier for the public to band together to promote reform legislation. State governments—where many politicians learn their craft—have always served as experimental grounds for democracy. As I described in chapter 2, Maine and Vermont have already passed legislation based on the idea of Clean Money

Campaign Reform, and legislators in at least six other states are poised to follow.

Clean Money Campaign Reform is the best working model of meaningful reform that I know of. I am 100 percent behind it. As I described in chapter 2, it provides a constitutionally acceptable option of full public financing for candidates who do not want to dirty their hands with special interest money. Let me briefly reiterate how it works: Candidates who can prove (by raising a specified number of small contributions) that they have popular support and who agree to not raise or spend any campaign money from private sources are eligible for public financing, which they receive not as a cash stipend but as an easy-to-monitor line of credit. This is the essence of Clean Money Campaign Reform: it creates a level playing field for all eligible candidates, breaks the hold that special interests have over our political process, closes existing loopholes, and is easily enforced.

In 1997, a federal Clean Elections bill was introduced by Senators John Glenn (D-OH), John Kerry (D-MA), and Paul Wellstone (D-MN). It is a bill that I support, and it is the only solution that lives up to the democratic ideals that we Americans value so much. But I've no illusion that it will get anywhere in Congress until there is a demand for it in a majority of the states and until enough angry people in the states take the battle to Congress.

Before I discuss ways in which we can build a movement in the states for Clean Money reform, let me mention a couple of interim reforms that, even under current political conditions, might win majority support in Congress.

First, we have to push Congress into enforcing—not ignoring—the current laws. We have got to push Congress into revamping the Federal Election Commission (FEC) and allowing it to do its job. As currently constituted, the FEC is unable to do its job. At full strength, it has three Republican and three Democratic commissioners who ensure that difficult decisions are avoided. Everything controversial ends in a tie. Consequently, hardly anything ever happens. One of the best solutions would be to change the FEC from a bipartisan to a nonpartisan commission. Give it independent leadership and a permanent professional staff and let it oversee federal elections without any interference from the president or Congress.

The Center for Responsive Politics (CRP) has done an excellent study of the Federal Election Commission and suggests the following reforms, all of which I endorse and all of which, if passed by Congress, would improve our campaign finance system and pave the way for more comprehensive reform like the Clean Money Campaign Reform. The CRP suggests that we

1. *Create an independent, nonpartisan agency led by people committed to law enforcement.* The agency should be headed by an odd-numbered commission, all of whose members are appointed by the president. Commissioners would be nominated by a non-partisan, blue-ribbon advisory panel. They could serve only one term.

2. *Insulate agency decisions from political pressures and the control of those whom the agency regulates.*

3. *Provide the agency with resources and enforcement authority.* The agency should have the authority to carry out field audits, conduct investigations, and impose sanctions.

4. *Create an agency that, by its ability to satisfactorily fulfill all of these objectives, would restore public confidence in the integrity of the election process.*

Another important reform the CRP recommends is in the area of disclosure. It's too easy for campaigns to disguise the identities of the special interests who give them money. It's too easy for special interests to disguise their intent with fine, patriotic-sounding names. And what good is it for the public to learn *after* the election is over that candidate "x" received $20,000 for his campaign from an oil company, a defense manufacturer, an insurance company, the tobacco industry, or a labor union?

130

Computers and the Internet make *instant* disclosure possible. A contribution received by a campaign on a Tuesday ought to become public by Wednesday and ought to be posted on the World Wide Web and in all appropriate media so that anyone who is interested in that campaign—journalists as well as members of the public—has access to that information. We have the technology; if we, the people, have the will, it will surely happen.

A further area of interim reform has to do with free media, as discussed in the second chapter. We need to fight to take back the airwaves. We, the public, own those airwaves and we should insist that the broadcast media fulfill their responsibility to offer election-time programming in the public interest. Of course, broadcasters are going to resist this. The communications industry is one of America's most successful and profitable industries. Entertainment is one of our great exports. American technology has always set the world standard. In movies, radio, television, computers, and now telecommunications, we lead the world.

The communications industry has never been shy about promoting itself. It has also never been shy about milking the government for the sake of its own self-interest. That is what communication is: promoting a case. Ironically, the industry has never relied on its own communicative skills to make its case. It has relied on the large amounts of money it gives political candidates and the two major parties.

Corporations involved with media, entertainment, telecommunications, and computers gave almost $23.7 million directly to congressional candidates during the 1996 election. They gave an additional $22.1 million in soft money to both political parties.

Because the television industry has invested heavily in Congress and the presidency over the years, it has effectively stripped the Federal Communications Commission (FCC) of its regulatory power. Recall our earlier discussion about ownership of the public airwaves. Before 1927, the airwaves were unregulated. The free market almost destroyed the industry before it got started: competing stations often blocked out each other's signals. Government intervention was necessary in order to end the static.

In 1927, the federal government stepped in and brought order to the airwaves, allocating licenses at specified frequencies. In return for their license to broadcast, radio stations had to agree to operate their stations in the public trust (television stations were licensed under the same requirement). We have the legal power to demand that broadcasters fulfill that minimal requirement.

I know about broadcast stations and profitability. I controlled a public company with sixteen radio stations. Compared to the three major networks and Fox Television, we were small. But because of my experience, I am qualified to say that the broadcast stations would not be financially harmed by being required to provide free political air time. My company could afford to give candidates and political parties free time to present their messages to the public, and if we could, then so can other television and radio stations.

Every European democracy gives candidates and their parties free time to present their messages. Free media should not be a controversial issue. Broadcaster greed makes it an issue and broadcaster money prevents it from happening.

In addition to pushing for free media, the public has to demand that Congress reinstate the Fairness Doctrine, which, in its final form, required that broadcasters devote comparable time for opposing viewpoints expressed by the station. Thus, if a station editorialized against abortion it would have to provide reasonable response time to a spokesperson for the pro-choice side.

In 1969, the legality of the Fairness Doctrine was upheld by the Court in *Red Lion Broadcasting Co. v. FCC*, which again emphasized the public's First Amendment rights over those of the broadcasters'. The ruling stated, "It is the purpose of the first amendment to preserve an uninhibited marketplace of ideas . . . rather than to countenance monopolization of the market." Thus, the ruling continued, "it is the right of the viewers and listeners, not the right of the broadcasters, which is paramount."

The "public interest" was undermined by the Reagan administration's free market economic policies and by the political contributions many congressional Democrats accepted. In 1987, the FCC unanimously voted to stop enforcing the Fairness Doctrine. The ruling stated that the doctrine was administrative law and so did not have the protection of congressional legislation. Congress, still controlled by the Democrats, immediately voted to enact the doctrine into law, but because many Democrats voted with the Reagan administration, supporters of the doctrine lacked the votes to override Reagan's presidential veto.

As things now stand, radio and television stations are under no obligation to provide balanced airtime. To be sure, the media make a great deal of noise about the occasional candidate debates they voluntarily cover. In effect, broadcasters present as an act of generosity something that should have been a public obligation required upon being granted a license.

We must raise the issue of public interest and insist that radio and television provide candidates and their parties free time to promote and discuss their political ideas. We must also insist that the Fairness Doctrine be reinstituted and that the media provide additional time for candidate debates and other informational programs.

In the long run, however, we need comprehensive reform, a Clean Money system in which a candidate's ideas, character, and leadership qualities are the decisive components—not the amount of money he or she can raise or spend in the quest for office.

Chapter Twelve

A Call to Arms: What You Can Do Today

During the last year, I have been working with computer program designers and the nonprofit groups pushing for campaign finance reform. Early on, I helped create a dynamic web site that features a petition drive to mobilize public opinion behind the Clean Money Campaign Reform and to let Congress know that momentum for reform is building.

Visit <www.publicampaign.org.> Take part in this very important drive by signing the petition, a Call for Real Reform. You can also participate if you do not have Internet access. Simply phone, toll-free, 1-888-293-5755, and have Public Campaign send you a kit that includes the Call for Real Reform petition. It is easy. It is important. And if enough of us get involved, it will work. I believe that through advertising and word-of-mouth, the petition drive can attract millions of people. Then you will see Congress scurrying.

Public Campaign, Common Cause, and other organizations can also put you in touch with organizations working at the state and local levels on Clean Money Campaign Reform. If we can build strength in the states—if a couple of other states pass legislation similar to that which passed in Maine and Vermont—we can go to Congress with momentum behind us.

What we must do is show Congress that we are damned angry. We need to make members understand that reforming the system is better than leaving it the way it is. That is the most effective and important route toward reform. The only way Congress will learn that there is a penalty for inaction is if we make it so. That is just the first part, though.

The pressure of public opinion is the route to success: letters, telegrams, telephone calls, e-mails, the petition drive (http://www.publicampaign.org), and most important of all, votes for candidates advocating reform but not for those who support the status quo. It will take more than one election, so we must start right away.

One final point: Although the issue is campaign finance reform, what we are really talking about is tax policy, balancing the budget, reforming the health insurance system, creating jobs and economic opportunity, protecting the environment, doing all the essential things that government does—not just for a small elite, but for all the people, the public, the nation. Clean Money Campaign Reform is the one reform that can make other reforms happen.

I held office as a Democrat, but I consider myself an Independent. The late Barry Goldwater, a Republican, summarized the argument for reform as well as any other politician. "The sheer cost of running for office is having a corrosive effect not only on American politics but on the quality of American government," he once said. "Something must be done to liberate candidates from their dependency on special interest money."

The Clean Money Campaign Reform that I am proposing is long overdue. Together we can make the states and the federal government bow to the demands of grassroots pressure and once again work for the people.